Y0-DNN-981

Study Guide
to
Prayer
Book
Spirituality

Study Guide to Prayer Book Spirituality

Dan Thomas Edwards

THE CHURCH HYMNAL CORPORATION, NEW YORK

Copyright © 1990
The Church Pension Fund
All rights reserved.

The Church Hymnal Corporation
800 Second Avenue
New York, NY 10017

5 4 3 2 1

Contents

Preface

The preparation of this guide has proved to be a delightful occasion for bringing together insights from diverse resources into a synthesis centered around *The Book of Common Prayer*. It is my hope that students and readers of *Prayer Book Spirituality* will find the *Study Guide* to be thought provoking and constructive for their personal spiritual practice and their participation in the corporate spirituality of the Anglican Communion.

I wish to thank J. Robert Wright, D. Phil. for his advisory role in *Study Guide to Prayer Book Spirituality*. The development of a study guide followed the popular acceptance of Rev. Wright's anthology of classical commentary on the Prayer Book. I have had the privilege to develop this guide under his supervision. Without Rev. Wright's guidance, constructive criticism, and editing, the writing of the study guide would not have been possible.

Dan Thomas Edwards
General Theological Seminary
New York, New York
April, 1990

Introduction

Prayer Book Spirituality by J. Robert Wright is an anthology of excerpts from theological and devotional commentaries on the *Book Of Common Prayer.* It is principally intended to serve as a devotional companion to the Prayer Book: In other words, its project is not formal or technical liturgical scholarship, but rather the enrichment of the devotional and even theological experience of those who worship according to the Prayer Book rites. It contains a wealth of information about the ways in which Anglicans have experienced and reflected upon *The Book Of Common Prayer* over the first 300 years of its use.

There are many creative approaches available for a course of study using this anthology. The book may, of course, be studied independently. However, the study could also be enriched by using *Prayer Book Spirituality* as the centerpiece of a broader course including a supplemental text. For example, the class could deal with the subject of Anglican identity using Sykes and Booty's *The Study Of Anglicanism.* [1] Another option would be to couple this text with Wolf's *Anglican Spirituality;* [2] Jones and Hosmer's *Living In The Spirit;* [3] or Thornton's *English Spirituality* [4] to explore ascetic theology and spiritual practice in the Anglican tradition.

A third option would be to join this study of devotional commentaries with a scholarly study of *The Book Of Common Prayer* itself, using a text such as Mitchell's *Praying Shapes Believing.* [5] A *via media* between the last two options would be to combine this historical anthology with a modern text on liturgical spirituality, such as Underhill's *Worship* [6] This choice is particularly interesting as it would supplement the twentieth-century perspective, and allow a woman's voice to be heard. Prof. Wright had noted his regret that there were no women writing in the genre of commentaries on the Prayer Book during this earlier period, and this deficiency would be somewhat ameliorated by considering Evelyn Underhill's study of the related topic of the nature of worship. This end is also served to some extent by Sr. Rachel Hosmer's contributions to *Living In The Spirit.*

If the class elects to study *Prayer Book Spirituality* independent of any other main text, the course may be enriched by reference to excerpts from a number of other sources. The commentaries and proposed discussion questions in this study guide cite a number of such sources. It is suggested that the instructor become familiar with these citations in advance, and that one or more of the students be assigned the supplemental reading so that their reports may enhance class discussion. Reading of supplemental sources in the fields of theology, psychology, spirituality, and contemporary liturgy is particularly recommended. Reading about historical antecedents to the Prayer Book may or may not serve the goals of the class depending on the focus of the course.

The use of *Study Guide* will depend on how the instructor chooses to structure the course. The *Study Guide* itself will address *Prayer Book Spirituality* on a chapter-by-chapter basis, as this is the format most likely to prove convenient to instructors or students, no matter how the course is structured. Some essential historical context will be provided in order to clarify the concerns that motivated the excerpted authors. Major themes connecting the different selections are included. (These themes are by no means exhaustive, and the student should be encouraged to identify other themes and concerns recurring in the different excerpts.) Finally, possible group-discussion questions are listed. Our intent is to provide a guide that will elucidate the text by providing historical and theological context, and help students see how the anthologized materials fit into the larger picture of evolving modes of Anglican worship.

CHAPTER ONE:

On Prayer in Common

A. Historical Context

When Thomas Cranmer first compiled *The Book Of Common Prayer* in 1549, he was at once doing some very new things—returning to ancient customs long since abandoned, and continuing traditions that had never been interrupted since the first century. This mix of old and new will be explained more fully in succeeding chapters. For now, it is important to realize that the idea of the people of God, people of all social ranks, lay and clergy alike, gathering frequently to hear the Scriptures read in their own language and to pray together in their own language, was a bold departure from medieval worship.

During the late Middle Ages, Scripture reading did not play an important role in the devotional life of the laity, and public prayers were generally recited by priests alone, in Latin. Cranmer's Book was dramatic change from late-medieval Roman Catholic liturgy; yet it was even more dramatically different from the new Calvinist liturgies that made sermons the central focus of worship, at the expense of Psalmody, corporate prayer, and Scripture reading.

Not surprisingly, the idea of common prayer met with some opposition. A rising Puritan protest objected to common prayer because it followed fixed forms that often resembled the forms used by the Roman church. The Puritans favored the spontaneity and variety of "extempore prayer" and the greater edification afforded by preaching. Their goal was to reform the Church of England along lines similar to Calvin's Church in Geneva. Much of Chapter One is comprised of Anglican defenses of common prayer per se (i.e., pray-

ers in which the whole assembly could join either by corporate recitation or by an informed "amen" in that they knew the prayers from
prior reading) against the Puritan critique of the sixteenth and seventeenth centuries. The Puritan Controversy (which included disputes
over church order as well as forms of worship) culminated in Civil
War and the banning of the Prayer Book during Oliver Cromwell's
Commonwealth until the Restoration of the monarchy.

B. Major Themes

The first major theme (which will reappear in Chapter Two) is that
common prayer expresses the unity of the Church and the communion of all the saints. The reader will see this theme running through
the passages from Hooker, Thorndike, Brevint, and Johnson. The
highest claim for this practice is advanced by Hooker as he associates
common prayer with the ongoing corporate prayers of saints and
angels in heaven. This claim is reiterated by Durel in Chapter Two,
pp.71–72. Hooker suggests that corporate prayer is (to use a term
characteristic of Hooker) a "participation" in Heavenly worship. See
also Comber at p.39. Hooker's claim is derived from Augustine's
portrait of Heavenly life in *The City of God,* Book XXII, Chs. 29, 30.[1]
See also, Isaiah 6 and Revelation 19, the scriptural texts cited by
Durel in Chapter Two.

A second theme is the honor to God done by consecrating a space
to God's glory and gathering publicly to worship. This theme con-
nects the readings from Herbert, Sparrow, and *The Whole Duty
Of Man.*

Third, several of the writers stress the spirituality of common
prayer for the common good of humankind rather than private prayer
which, if not balanced with corporate prayer, tends toward a self-
centered spirituality. This theme is particularly important to contrast
Anglican spirituality with the privatism of spiritualities since the
Great Awakening. To reflect on the theological dimension of this
theme, it may be helpful to consider the theology of J. B. Metz. For
a concise summary of Metz's perspective on the social dimension of
grace, see Carpenter, *Nature & Grace.*[2] To reflect on the spiritual
dimension of this theme, it may be helpful to consider Stevick,

12

"The Spirituality Of The Book Of Common Prayer," in *Anglican Spirituality* at pp.114–117.[3] It may be constructive to observe the use of the first person plural in the Prayer Book. This theme is most apparent in the excerpts from Herbert, Sparrow, and Horneck.

Fourth, Comber argues that common prayer according to fixed forms is superior to extempore prayer as a means to heartfelt worship. This theme appears more prominently in Chapter Two. Hobart's and Comber's concern for postures in the pews may be related to this goal of common prayer.

C. For Discussion

The study and discussion of this topic may be greatly enhanced by reading at least the first chapter of Weil, *Gathered To Pray*.[4] The first major theme of Chapter Two in *Prayer Book Spirituality* is also particularly addressed by Weil at p.16. Both *Gathered To Pray* and Thornton's *English Spirituality* are helpful in considering the respective roles of corporate and private prayer in a total spiritual practice.

1. Read Isaiah 6 and Revelation 19. These texts do not prescribe specific liturgical forms. However, they do portray the heavenly life as one of corporate prayer and praise. Does this portrait of our divine destiny tell us anything about how we should live and worship in the present?

2. The Puritans protested that prayer should come spontaneously from the heart. The Anglicans were more concerned about helping people to pray together, and that goal required fixed forms. Should there be a place for extemporaneous prayer in public worship? In private devotions? Should there be a place for fixed-form prayers in public worship? In private devotions?

3. Anglicans and Puritans alike sought to ground worship in Scripture, but Puritans went further in excluding ancient prayers of the early church. Does the antiquity of a prayer or the identity of its author contribute to its devotional value? If so, how?

4. What is the spiritual, theological, and ecclesiological significance of two or more Christians praying together?

5. In the Nicene Creed, we affirm our belief in "one, holy, catholic, and apostolic Church." The concept of "apostolicity" is related to continuing in the same tradition of teaching and mission as the apostles. The historic episcopate is one symbol of this continuity.[5] Does continuing in the prayer forms of the early church also relate to this idea of "apostolicity"?

6. What do you make of Herbert's housekeeping concerns and Hobart's worry over prayer postures? Do these texts reflect a petty fussiness and materialism? Herbert was one of England's greatest poets, and Hobart was one of America's greatest bishops. What could be valuable about such attention to detail? What could be negative about such attention to detail?

On Prayer from a Book

A. Historical Context

The issues of common prayer and prayer according to fixed forms were intimately related, as fixed forms were the means-to-the-end of truly common prayer. So the historical context is essentially the same in this chapter as in Chapter One. The particular texts included in Chapter Two may be elucidated by some additional detail. Part of Cranmer's method was to purge Anglican liturgy of those medieval developments in worship that were regarded as "corruptions." The liturgical practices and doctrines of the first five centuries of Church history, however, were still regarded as authoritative. The clearest statement of that position was the Act of Uniformity in 1559, which acknowledged the authority of the first four ecumenical councils, but not of any subsequent council of the Church. This deference to the practices of antiquity became a fundamental element of the defense of fixed forms for prayer.

Chapter Two includes more material from the eighteenth and early nineteenth centuries than we saw in Chapter One. During the Age of Reason, Anglicanism's first great apologist was John Locke, who argued for a "reasonable religion" in contrast to the religious fervor that had led to the excesses of religious warfare since the mid-sixteenth century. Later it fell to Joseph Butler to defend the reasonableness of Anglican faith as against the more skeptical and rationalist Deism movement. This claim to reasonableness is reflected in concerns for agreement, decency, and order, dignity and propriety of language, and, most explicitly, "a reasonable and enlightened service."

The reader may find that some of the values of the seventeenth- and eighteenth-century writers seem stuffy and rigid, by our standards; but such a judgment would fail to grasp the spirit and perspective of the Enlightenment. As a reaction against the religious warfare that had ravaged Europe in the aftermath of the Reformation, and in response to the Newtonian science of the day, it was an age that valued order and dignity. Such order was the mark of God's will in nature and human affairs. The music, art, and literature of the time display an aesthetic of orderliness unparalleled since Greek culture of the fifth century B.C.E. It seemed appropriate to the Anglican apologists that God should be honored in aesthetic expressions consonant with the aesthetic values of the time.

Yet the eighteenth century was also the time of the Great Awakening and the evangelical movement. In response, some Anglicans stressed the superiority of "true and sincere devotion" over "seeming fervor," but others claimed that the Prayer Book services were indeed "evangelical worship." The student may wish to note the extent to which Anglican apologetics dealt with Puritanism, Deism, and the Evangelical movement by a degree of accommodation (i.e., justifying Prayer Book worship by the standards of these three movements) and by a degree of refutation.

B. Major Themes

Many of the central themes of this chapter are aptly captured in the excerpt from Brownell, pp.100–111 and in Beveridge's witty criticism of extemporaneous prayer on p.75. The student may wish to read these passages first.

The first theme is the justification of fixed-form prayers by reference to the practices of the early church. This theme is prominent in the passages from Hooker, *Eikon Basilike,* Durel, Secker, Hobart, and Brownell. This argument reflects Hooker's theological principle that, in matters not essential to salvation (including forms of worship and church order), it is sufficient authority that a practice is not contrary to Scripture and that it is reasonable as attested by ancient usage. This method was set against the Puritan insistence that the Church should do nothing that was not clearly authorized by Scripture.

16

However, the second theme is an attempt to justify fixed-form prayer according to the Puritan standard: appeal to Scripture itself. Durel, Beveridge, Secker, and Brownell claim Scriptural warrant for the general principle of fixed forms of worship. Beveridge, Johnson, and Secker even turned the Puritan method to their advantage, relying on Matthew 18:19 to argue that it is essential to biblically sound prayer that the content of the prayer be agreed upon beforehand, and that extemporaneous prayer failed this test.

A third prominent theme is the value of fixed-form prayers for edification and instruction. Puritans claimed that the sermon and extemporaneous prayer were "more edifying" than Prayer Book services. Durel, Hobart, Secker, and Brownell argued that repeated usage of prayers that contained and constituted a "standard of faith" was more edifying. To fully grasp the concern for edification, the student should think of edification not as a purely cognitive enterprise, but rather as spiritual formation of the whole person.

In Chapter One, we read Comber's claim that fixed-form prayers are actually more effective for inspiring fervent devotion. That theme is elaborated here in the works of Beveridge, Secker, and Brownell. Also in Chapter One, we read texts expressing the concern that public worship should be done in a manner that would honor God. This concern is elaborated here by commitments to beauty, dignity, decency and order, clarity and propriety. These characteristics of worship were offered as an alternative to "seeming fervor" as fitting ways to glorify God. This theme is prominent in the texts from Bisse, Hobart, and Brownell.

C. For Discussion

1. Check the scriptural authorities relied upon by the authors who attempted to justify fixed-form prayers by appeal to Scripture. To what extent do the biblical texts really support the use of fixed-form prayers? To what extent do these texts support the forms used in *The Book of Common Prayer?*

2. At various times since the Reformation, liturgical scholars have engaged in vigorous debates as to what the liturgical practices actu-

ally were in the early church. We may grant that some fixed forms of prayers were common in the early church, but many of our collects are of more recent origin. Moreover, as for specific liturgical customs in the early church, it appears that practices were often different in different communities. For example, some anointed before water baptism, some anointed after water baptism, and some anointed before and after water baptism.

Uniformity developed gradually. The early church therefore does not provide a single, clear prescription for forms of worship. In light of this fact, to what extent are we bound to the forms of the early church? To what extent are we free to cast them aside and devise new forms to fit modern culture? What is lost and what is gained in either case?

3. Three of these authors justify the use of fixed-form prayers by the fact that the people have somehow agreed upon these prayers in advance. In what sense is this really the case? Is our agreement through the agency of those who approved the Prayer Book? Does one agree to the prayers more personally, after having heard them repeatedly, by then continuing in Prayer Book worship? Can an agreement be found in the Baptismal Covenant at p.304 of *The Book Of Common Prayer?*

4. The apologists in this chapter placed great stress on dignity, order, propriety, and other such arguably aesthetic values. Others emphasized subjective feelings of the worshipers. To what extent is the purpose of worship to honor God? To what extent is it to contribute to the spiritual formation of the worshipers? How do we determine what manner of worship pleases God? How do we determine what manner of worship contributes to spiritual formation? Why not just do whatever people like?

5. Is a subjective feeling of excitement necessarily the same thing as an experience of the Holy Spirit? Can the Spirit be present in something quiet? Even something dull? What does I Kings 19:9–13 suggest? What is the place of emotion in spiritual formation?

CHAPTER THREE:

The Calendar and Liturgical Year

A. Historical Context

The observance of liturgical seasons began early in church history, and the details of how this practice began and evolved have been the subject of some fascinating liturgical detective work. Students who wish to explore this subject in greater depth could not turn to a better source than Talley, *The Origins Of The Liturgical Year.* [1] A more concise account of the observance of the holy seasons may be found in Cobb, "The History Of The Christian Year," in *The Study Of Liturgy.* [2]

The observance of these seasons and holy days soon came to be supplemented by commemoration of the births and deaths of martyrs and other saints. Over the course of the Middle Ages, the number of saints and the legends extolling them proliferated, and the cult of martyrs came to be attended by superstition and abusive practices relating to relics. This led to severe criticism of the cult by such early reformers as Wycliffe and Gerson, then later by the humanists such as Erasmus. For a concise account of the medieval veneration of saints, the student may consult Donovan, "The Sanctoral," also in *The Study Of Liturgy.* [3]

The Protestant Reformation on the Continent rejected the veneration of saints, and the observance of holy days fell into disfavor by association. Cranmer had drastically curtailed the number of holy days to be observed; but the Puritans felt that he had not gone nearly far enough. Puritans objected that holy days were occasions for idleness and tended toward superstition as a result of the medieval abuses. They contended that the Christian duty was to honor God always, not merely on special days. They further objected to such observances on the grounds of their similarity to the practices of Judaism and Roman Catholicism. During the reign of Cromwell, the Puritan-dominated Commonwealth even abolished the observance of Christmas. The excerpts anthologized in this chapter defend the observance of the liturgical year against Puritan criticisms, and instruct Anglicans in a nonsuperstitious piety that is served by the setting aside of special days for special meditations and reflections.

In order to better understand the role of the liturgical week and year in contemporary Anglican piety, the student may wish to read Mitchell, *Praying Shapes Believing,* Chapter Two.[4] The related concept of "sabbath time," is beautifully and concisely treated in Chapter Three of Edwards's *Spiritual Friend.*[5]

B. Major Themes

The themes of each of the writers in this chapter are uniform and straightforward. The observance of holy seasons and holy days are a reasonable and efficacious means to honor God and to remind Christians of God's mercies shown in salvation history. The commemoration of the lives of the saints is not an idolatrous worship of the saints, but rather a thanksgiving for "the graces of God which did shine in those departed souls."

Holy days are not an occasion for idleness, but rather for religious exercises the purpose of which is the glorification of God and the salvation of the souls of worshipers. The justification of holy days as a means to instruct members in history and doctrine as well as to excite their celebration of infinite love parallels the themes of instruction and devotion in Chapter Two, and may be understood in terms of a spiritual formation of the whole person.

C. For Discussion

1. The Christian year fixes Lent and Advent as penitential seasons. Is there room in those seasons for the experience and expression of Christian joy? How can this be done without undermining the theme of the season?

2. Conversely, Christmas and Easter are joyous seasons. Is there room for contrition at those times?

3. In this chapter, the writers deal with the sanctifying or consecrating of certain times to the glory of God. In Chapter One, some writers (Herbert, for one) dealt with setting aside certain places for proclaiming the glory of God. Puritans objected to setting aside either special times or special places. Anglicans wished to set aside special times and special places. Are these issues related? What does it say about the difference in the two approaches to life and faith?

4. Does setting aside certain days as sacred suggest that other days are profane? In other words, does it invite Christians to view their faith as a matter of concern only on Sundays and special holy days, leaving faith segregated from most of their life?

5. The sanctification of space and time has been noted by anthropologists in many religions. Read Chapters One and Two of Eliade's *The Sacred And The Profane*. [6] In light of the anthropological insights concerning space and time, is the consecration of churches and the liturgical structuring of the year fundamental to religious experience? Or is the mythical perspective that Eliade describes mere "superstition" which should be overcome by more rational religion?

6. What does Tilden Edwards's concept of sabbath time teach us about the observance of holy days, or about the observance of holiness in each day?

7. Read McClendon's *Biography As Theology,* at least Chapter Seven and the Appendix "Christian Worship And The Saints." [7] What is the value of reflecting upon the lives of notable Christians in the spiritual formation of the modern Christian?

CHAPTER FOUR:

The Daily Office

A. Historical Context

Jewish temple worship in the Old Testament followed the mandate of Exodus 29:38–42 to offer daily holocaust sacrifices at dawn and sunset. Our knowledge of Jewish worship in the first century C.E. is limited, but we do know that there is a long tradition of meeting in the synagogue three times each day for Scripture reading and prayer. The earliest Christian book of church order, the *Didache,* prescribes recitation of the Lord's Prayer three times daily. Other sources on the prayer practices of the early church suggest that the people gathered for common prayer at fixed hours each day, and that other fixed hours were prescribed for private or family prayers.[1]

During the Middle Ages, these prayers, which came to be known as the divine office or the liturgy of the hours, became more and more elaborate. The occasions of common prayer were set at seven hours of the day, and variations for seasons and holy days became too complex for the secular clergy to recall by heart. In the eleventh century, this increased complexity required the publication of the first breviaries which were the literary precursor to the Prayer Book. Despite the advent of breviaries, the actual gathering for daily prayer became more and more limited to monasteries. The laity and secular clergy either failed to observe the hours, or they observed them privately.[2]

Cranmer probably began working on an Anglican Daily Office in 1538, though his first Prayer Book was not published until 1549. His Preface to the first Prayer Book (the student would do well to read this Preface) deals almost entirely with the Daily Office, indicating its importance in the emerging Anglican spirituality. His project was essentially twofold: first, to abridge and simplify the Daily Office so that it would be practical for the laity to observe the prayers faithfully; and second, to structure the Office around the reading of Scripture so that the people, who had only recently gained access to the Bible in their own language, might be thoroughly immersed in biblical religion. He accomplished these goals by composing two streamlined services, Morning Prayer and Evening Prayer, each containing substantial readings of Scripture.

The 1552 Prayer Book made one significant change. It added the Exhortation to Confession, the General Confession, and the Absolution at the beginning of each service.[3] Martin Thornton, the leading scholar of English ascetic theology and practice, has observed that the Prayer Book Daily Office reflects two dominant influences: one, the prayers and practices of the early church; and two, Benedictine spirituality, indicating the influence of Benedictines in English religious life since St. Augustine of Canterbury, himself a Benedictine, reunited the Church of England to the rest of Christendom in 597 C.E.[4]

Students not familiar with Morning and Evening Prayer may benefit from reading the Associated Parishes publication *The Daily Office: A Guide For Individual And Group Recitation.*[5] An excellent discussion of the role of the Daily Office as a part of a comprehensive spiritual practice appears in Thornton, *English Spirituality*, Chapter 20.[6] Thornton argues,

> *Thus the elimination of the Office diminishes our sense of the divine transcendence and usually issues in some form of spiritual eudemonism: subjectivism, sentimentality, pantheism, Quietism, and the like. The elimination of personal devotion inspired by the indwelling Spirit leads to the opposite errors: legalism, formalism, and all the dangers of the Pharisees.*[7]

Students may also gain a deeper understanding of the spiritual value of community devotions by reading Chapter Two of Bonhoeffer's *Life Together.*[8] The best guide to the contemporary observance of the Daily Office and the associated piety is perhaps Mitchell's *Praying Shapes Believing*, Chapter Three.[9]

B. Major Themes

The first major theme that appears in the anthologized excerpts is the unity of humanity represented by the corporate Daily Office and the reorientation of the worshiper's affections from self-centeredness to concern for the neighbor. This theme appears in Andrewes's and Maurice's reflections on the Lord's Prayer and in Sparrow's reflection on the Divine Salutation.

A related but broader theme is the role of the Daily Office in spiritual formation. This appears in Andrewes's stress on sanctification; Comber's observance of how the Office elevates the soul "to contemplate the Beauties of the Divine Nature . . . and delight to imitate so excellent and great a Pattern"; Hooker's recounting the virtues exemplified in the Psalms; and Johnson's view of the Offices as teaching a positive holiness in which the Christian is "devoted to God, to be like him." The student who wishes to explore more deeply the theological basis for such a spirituality should read Allchin's *Participation In God.* [10]

The third major theme relates to the 1549 addition of a penitential introduction to Morning and Evening Prayer. Comber, Johnson, Secker, Hobart, and Simeon place major emphasis on the penitential element of these services. Concerning this theme, the student would do well to read Booty's "Contrition In Anglican Spirituality," in *Anglican Spirituality.* [11]

C. For Discussion

1. The *hesychast* tradition in Eastern Orthodoxy is based on spiritual formation by frequent repetition of the Jesus Prayer. How is the daily recitation of the Daily Office similar to the practice of the Jesus Prayer? How is it different?

2. Simone Weil experienced a profound conversion through attentively reciting the Lord's Prayer. In *Waiting For God,* she maintains that one cannot attentively pray these words without undergoing a real change of soul.[12] Do you agree with Maurice that we ordinarily lack the capacity to pray these words sincerely? If we pray the Lord's

Prayer sincerely and attentively, what manner of conversion of our hearts might occur? Is the ability to pray this prayer a virtue to be achieved through practice, a matter of grace, or a combination of the two?

3. What role should contrition or penitence play in a healthy spirituality? Is religious penitence a destructive, unhealthy assault on self-esteem? Or is it an essential response to both real and neurotic guilt? The student may gain some excellent insights into these issues by reading the Ulanovs' *Primary Speech,* Chapter One.[13]

4. Does corporate confession imply a belief in corporate sin as in shared social responsibility for social evils? Is corporate confession also a proper means of addressing personal sins? Is it adequate?

5. Hooker's account of the Psalms as a portrayal of a wealth of virtues is only a partial account. The Psalms include sentiments of vindictiveness, self-righteousness, self-pity, and despair. Is there value in reciting poetic expressions of these less virtuous sentiments? If so, what? Review Chapter One of *Primary Speech.* Does the Ulanovs' view of prayer help to answer these present questions?

CHAPTER FIVE

The Litany

A. Historical Context

Evelyn Underhill has noted:

> *The litany, or series of brief acts of prayer and praise with a fixed response, is, according to Heiler, one of the most archaic forms of common worship; and is still found in many tribal rituals. It is a simple and obvious device for securing the attention and united religious action of a group without service-books or ritual knowledge; for all the congregation needs to know is the choral response by which it endorses the leader's prayer. This choral response is always brief . . .*[1]

Some of the authors anthologized in Chapter Five stress the relative antiquity of the litany as a Christian liturgical form, though they are not sure that they can ground it in the authority of the venerable "patristic" era. It is, however, clear that the litany is a prayer structure of long-standing usage in Christianity, and that the *Kyrie* at the beginning of the Eucharist is a vestige of an earlier litany.

The litany has been called "the classic general intercession in the Prayer Book tradition" because it is "the only general intercession in the regular Sunday services . . . , for the Prayer for the Whole State of Christ's Church is a prayer for the Church only and not for the world."[2] This service may be performed independently, but it has more customarily been used as the introit for the Holy Eucharist or following the collects in Morning and Evening Prayer. Its penitential tone makes it particularly appropriate for Advent and Lent.[3] The Supplication at the end of the litany is provided for times of war or other disasters.[4]

The Anglican Great Litany was the first liturgical service in the

English language, having been published in 1544, and having then been included in every edition of the Prayer Book from 1549 forward.[5] The litany was criticized by the Puritans, but the passages in Chapter Five do not focus so much on the defense of the litany as on guiding worshipers to a better understanding of the nature of the prayer.

B. Major Themes

The first apparent theme is that the litany includes, and in some sense associates, prayers for ourselves and prayers for the well-being and deliverance of the whole world, including friends and enemies alike. This theme is prominent in each of the passages except Comber's.

A second theme is that the litany includes, and in some sense associates, prayers for deliverance from sin and deliverance from worldly adversity. This theme appears in each of the passages except Sparrow's (and the Maurice excerpt focuses on adversity rather than sin).

The interesting issue is how the authors relate these two kinds of petitions. Hobart forthrightly asserts that "the transgressions by which we offend God are the cause of our suffering." Comber regards worldly trials and tribulations as occasions that teach us the need of prayer, saying that when we are in trouble "then we are most fit to pray and he is most apt to hear us." But he goes on to say that we must "live holily as well as trust firmly," for otherwise we "have no right to his Promises nor reason to expect any deliverance . . ." Maurice takes yet a third view of "the actual vulgar sorrows to which flesh is heir" and which are the subject of the litany's petitions. He sees human suffering as the context in which human beings meet the Christ who has "actually entered into the depths of human sorrow," and regards the "press and tumult of life" as a teacher that instructs us as to how we should approach the divine altar.

A third theme, found in Hobart alone, is his reiteration of the propriety of kneeling for prayer.

C. For Discussion

1. In contrast to other Prayer Book services, the litany is dominated by petitions, supplications, and intercessions, to the virtual exclusion

of prayers of praise and thanksgiving. Does this make the litany a selfish, infantile, superstitious form of prayer? Or is it an acknowledgment of dependency on our Creator? Does honesty in prayer dictate that we begin in such supplications that are our most pressing concerns?

Read about desire and fear in Chapters Two and Four of *Primary Speech.* [6] What are the theological and psychological grounds for devoting substantial prayer time to the quest for one's own well-being and the well-being of one's community?

2. What good is actually done by prayers of intercession for others? Will God deliver those who would otherwise not be delivered because we have asked him to deliver them? Read *Worship* pp.150–153 and Chapter Nine of *Primary Speech.* [7] What are the theological and psychological grounds for prayers of intercession?

3. What do you think of the views of Secker, Comber, and Maurice regarding the relationship between sin and suffering? Read John 9:1–3 and Luke 13:1–5. In what sense are sin and suffering related? Does holy living give us a "right" to deliverance from worldly hardship?

4. What is the nature and role of God as suggested by the Great Litany? What is the world like? And what is the Christian's relationship to God and the world?

5. In the course of modern controversies over gender-inclusive language, some have proposed referring to God in Trinity as "Creator, Sanctifier, Redeemer." Others have regarded this terminology as contrary to our tradition. Some have considered such language "heretical." What do you make of the first three petitions of the litany as described by Sparrow? Is this an adequate way of speaking about God? Are there adequate ways for speaking about God? Are some ways more helpful (edifying) than others?

CHAPTER SIX

Christian Initiation

A. Historical Context

The rites of Christian initiation have undergone a long and complex history, with understandings of these rites varying dramatically from time to time and place to place. Conflicts over differing understandings of these rites have been intense, and have often represented differing understandings of the very heart of the Christian faith, the nature of the apostolic mission, and the role of the Christian in the social order. This *Study Guide* cannot even begin to survey such a history, but it is essential to point out that the excerpts in Chapter Six are a sampling of some views that have been held concerning Christian initiation, and are not intended to constitute a complete or authoritative statement of the Church's current understanding.[1]

The nature and forms of Baptism and Confirmation were subjects of debate during the Reformation and the Puritan Controversy. Some of the passages in Chapter Six are taken from polemical defenses of the Church of England's methods of initiation; however, the specific issues do not explicitly appear in these excerpts, with minor exceptions such as Durel's defense of the use of the sign of the cross.

Hobart's comments may need to be understood in light of his writing in the aftermath of the Second Great Awakening—a revival movement in which the importance of a personal conversion experience figured far more prominently than the sacrament of Baptism. And, indeed, the Awakenings in America had been attended by debates over whether one was a true member of the Church solely by virtue of Baptism, if one had not also undergone such an experience. This is not to say that Hobart's understanding of postbaptismal conversion and the rite of Confirmation was an original response to the Awakening. It was not. The Awakenings, however, were important influences on the religious climate in which he wrote and are therefore important to understanding the significance of his choice of these themes for his time.

Much has happened to the Anglican doctrine of Baptism since these passages were written. For example, John Henry Newman, leader of the Oxford Movement, argued for a higher view of Baptism, as being more significant for salvation, than did any of the writers anthologized here. Newman placed great emphasis on the salvific effect of regeneration or second birth, and took the New Testament characterization of Baptism as such a second birth quite seriously. On the other hand, the Broad Church Movement, exemplified by Frederick Denison Maurice, rejected the notion that Baptism separated the Christian from the ranks of the damned and placed him or her among the ranks of the blessed. Rather, in his view, Baptism was a sacramental expression of a relationship with Christ, having its basis in the creation and the atonement. Baptism expressed a relationship that already existed.[2]

The process of revising *The Book Of Common Prayer* for the American Church in the late 1970s involved extensive rethinking of the theology of Baptism and Confirmation. The student is strongly encouraged to read the Associated Parishes publication *Christian Initiation: A Theological And Pastoral Commentary On The Proposed Rite.*[3] This will provide a concise summary of much contemporary thinking on the subject of Christian initiation. (The word "contemporary" is subject to some question, since the intention of the revisions in the 1979 Prayer Book was to restore aspects of the early church's understanding of the rite.)

The same topic is explored, still concisely but in greater depth, in Chapter Five of *Praying Shapes Believing.*[4] The most important modern articulation of the doctrine of Christian initiation is perhaps the Lima statement of the World Council Of Churches, *Baptism, Eucharist, and Ministry.*[5] This is also a short text and is essential reading for anyone who wishes to grasp the modern understanding of Christian initiation.

Four points in particular should be gleaned from reading these modern texts, so that they may be compared to the views of the sixteenth- and seventeenth-century texts in Chapter Five: (a) Baptism is a complete initiation into the Body Of Christ which is the Church; (b) The bond established in Baptism is indissoluble; (c) Confirmation is a renewal rather than a completion of the baptismal covenant; (d) Baptism is unrepeatable, but should be constantly reaffirmed during the baptized Christian's "continuing struggle" and "continuing experience of grace."

B. Major Themes

Among the views of Baptism presented in Chapter Six, the differences predominate over the commonalities. For Jewel, Baptism is principally a washing in the blood of Christ to remove the stain of original sin. He thus implies a lostness prior to Baptism. Hooker sees Baptism rather as "a seal . . . to the grace of Election, before received, but to our sanctification here a step that hath not any before it." Thus for Hooker, the importance of Baptism is not to effect, so much as to commemorate, the justification that constitutes the person a child of God and heir to salvation. It is, more vitally, an initiation into the lifelong process of growth into holiness, which is not a means to salvation but rather the fruit of salvation. *The Whole Duty Of Man* regards Baptism chiefly as a matter of covenant. This is not a subtle insight. Clearly a covenant is formed at Baptism. The interesting dimension of *The Whole Duty* is its legalistic view of Baptism as a conditional covenant. "Unless we do indeed perform them (our vows), God is not tied to make good his, and so we forfeit all those precious Benefits and Advantages." Essentially, Baptism is the making of a contract whereby the Christian promises to live a holy life in exchange for salvation, and one who fails to keep his end of the bargain is "left in that natural and miserable Estate of ours, Children of Wrath, Enemies to God, and Heirs of eternal Damnation."

Hobart's view elaborates upon and enriches the doctrine of Baptism found in *The Whole Duty*, reaching a conclusion which is consistent with that of *The Whole Duty*. Hobart holds that, in Baptism, God pledges to the Christian the grace sufficient to enable "faith and evangelical obedience." The baptized Christian receives the grace to later experience "renovation, renewing, conversion, sanctification"; but that grace is not irresistible. For those who do not go on to experience such a growth into holiness, "the regeneration of Baptism will only increase the guilt and condemnation."

Durel stresses the function of Baptism as enrollment into a militia, a making of the new Christian as one who takes God's side against "the old man" whom he must crucify within himself. Comber sees Baptism as effecting internal regeneration (rebirth), which he associates with cleansing from original sin and external grafting into Christ's Church. The Holy Spirit is received at Baptism, but "greater measures of the Spirit" are received at Confirmation, and these are accompanied by spiritual gifts for the service of God. Patrick holds that Baptism is becoming a member of the Body of Christ. Confirmation is a ratification of the contract made on one's behalf and the receiving of a new grace to strengthen and confirm the Christian's good resolution to comply with the contract.

The propriety of infant Baptism is expressly addressed by some of these authors, and it is an implicit concern for all of them, particularly Hobart. Infant baptism was not a subject of Reformation debate (except for the Anabaptists); nor was it a dispute in the Puritan controversy; but the Protestant doctrine of salvation by faith necessitated a new effort to justify the Baptism of those too young to experience faith subjectively. Readers will do well to compare the different approaches of these authors in their efforts to reconcile infant Baptism with justification by faith. This may be considered through the asking of two questions: What does the author mean by "faith"? What, in the author's opinion, is the effect of Baptism for those who do not come to a subjective experience of God or intellectual assent to the doctrines of the Church?

C. For Discussion

1. Which of the authors anthologized in Chapter Six advances views most consistent with modern understandings of Christian initiation such as we find in the World Council of Churches agreement, *Baptism, Eucharist, and Ministry?* Which author is least consistent with modern doctrine?

2. The concern in *The Whole Duty Of Man* is to combat religious formalism (the idea that ritual compliance is all that is required for salvation, so belief and ethical conduct become irrelevant). The problem with the approach taken in *The Whole Duty* is a legalism that diminishes the significance of Baptism to an acknowledgment of natural duties to do good and recognize truth. This conflict reflects the theological difference between grace and works as they relate to salvation and the Christian life. How do you resolve this conflict? Is Baptism a curse and not a blessing for those who fail to grow in the Christian faith? Is Baptism an assurance of salvation? If so, does it render the rest of Christian life irrelevant and meaningless?

3. How is Baptism the beginning of sanctification? Does it make a real difference in the future life of Christians who are baptized as infants?

4. How would you compare Hooker's and Patrick's doctrines of Confirmation?

5. Read *The Sacred & The Profane,* pp.129–138.[6] From the standpoint of anthropology of religion and the standpoint of the early church, what does it mean to say one is regenerated or reborn in Baptism?

CHAPTER SEVEN:

The Holy Eucharist

The history of the various understandings and modes of Christian initiation was indeed long and complex; but the history of the various understandings and forms of celebration of the Holy Eucharist has been even more involved, and there have been even hotter debates on these topics. Accordingly, the materials presented in Chapter Seven are rather extensive and involved. This is necessary in order to offer a fair representation of the views of the Eucharist that were held by Anglicans during the time frame covered. The quantity of material on this subject is also consonant with the central importance of the Eucharist in Anglican worship. The length, complexity, and diversity of these materials, however, present the instructor with a pedagogical problem: How to manage these materials in such a way as to make them comprehensible rather than overwhelming.

The following suggestions may prove helpful:

1. Devote twice as much class time to the discussion of this chapter as you have devoted for the previous chapters. This will permit a fuller consideration of each discussion question to allow for the greater diversity of opinion included in the materials. It is necessary, however, for the students to have read materials covering the entire time frame before undertaking consideration of any of the discussion questions.

2. It may be unrealistic to expect all the students to read all the materials in Chapter Seven. Each of the excerpts is numbered. You might divide the group into halves, with one half reading the even-

numbered passages and the other half reading the odd-numbered passages. It is not recommended to have one group read the earlier texts and the other group read the later texts. It is better for each student to have an opportunity to gain some sense of how understandings of the Eucharist have evolved over time.

3. It may be helpful for the instructor or one of the students to give a presentation on contemporary understandings of the Eucharist, from theological and spiritual perspectives. This should give the class some framework for understanding the issues that shape the texts in the chapter.

American students may benefit from reading the Associated Parishes publications *Parish Eucharist* and *Holy Eucharist Rite Two: A Commentary.* [1] These pamphlets clarify the structure and basic theology of the contemporary American rites. *Baptism, Eucharist, and Ministry* is strongly recommended for all students, both in that it provides an ecumenical perspective, and in that it is a concise, very well-articulated statement of contemporary theology of the Eucharist. [2] It regards the Eucharist as a thanksgiving to the Father, an *anamnesis* or memorial of Christ, an invocation of the Spirit, a communion of the faithful, and a meal of the kingdom. The image of memorial (a traditionally Protestant image) is elaborated to include not only a remembrance, but also intercession and sacrifice of ourselves. This accommodates the image of the Eucharist as a propitiatory sacrifice, an image traditionally associated with Roman Catholic theology.

Underhill similarly espoused multiple complementary images to portray the meaning of the Eucharist, stating,

> *We . . . ask what this, the greatest of all Christian acts of worship with its unchanging centre, and many kinds and degrees of outward expression, has meant and means for Christian devotion. Where does, and where should, its true emphasis lie? Which of the many strands that are united in it should be given priority? . . . The answer is that no view can be adequate which neglects any of these meanings.* [3]

Students who wish to examine the separate movements, prayers, and actions that cumulatively make up the eucharistic rite, will find a helpful theological analysis in *Praying Shapes Believing,* Chapter Six. [4]

A. Historical Context

Biblical and liturgical scholars debate the relationship between the institution of the Eucharist and early Jewish liturgies such as the Passover meal, the sacrificial rites, and blessings before ordinary meals. A cursory summary of some of these issues may be found in Berkhoff, *Christian Faith.* [5] It is clear, however, that these Jewish precedents influenced the understanding of the Eucharist in the early church. Another first-century custom may also have had some influence on the meaning of the Eucharist as the Church has understood it. That custom was the table fellowship practiced by Jesus and his disciples, not as formal liturgy but as celebration or banquet. Such table fellowship continued to play an important role in the Church of the Apostolic Age. Paul's admonitions in I Corinthians 11 suggest that the Eucharist occurred in the context of such a social table fellowship. Professor John Koenig argues in *New Testament Hospitality* that such banquets were metaphors of the abundance of the kingdom and that such hospitable gatherings were expressions of the Gospel as well as a primary context for communicating the Gospel. [6] This background may underlie our understanding of the Eucharist as a foretaste of the messianic banquet of Heaven.

The celebration of the Eucharist as a liturgical rite became separate from social table fellowship quite early; however, the Eucharist remained a central feature in the worship of the early church. The earliest detailed theological explanation of the Eucharist, after the New Testament, is from Justin Martyr in the mid-second century. Justin related that the bread and wine were transformed by the eucharistic Prayer into the Body and Blood of Christ; that the bread and cup were to be identified with the pure sacrifice described by Malachi; that the Eucharist was a memorial of the incarnation and passion of Christ; and that the Eucharist was a thanksgiving for creation and redemption. [7] Later patristic authorities were somewhat divided as to whether the consecration was effected by the "words of institution" (words used by Christ to institute the sacrament), the *epiklesis* (prayer invoking the Holy Spirit), or by the prayers as a whole. Eusebius and Cyril of Jerusalem taught that the Eucharist is an image of heavenly reality. [8]

The evolution of eucharistic theology and practice between the fourth century and the Protestant Reformation in the sixteenth century cannot be fairly summarized in a brief study guide, but some trends must be noted (even the description of these trends is grossly simplified) in order to make sense of the readings in Chapter Seven.

The post-Constantine status of the Church in the empire and the Arian controversies, both in the fourth century, marked a turning point. Christ came to be portrayed more as an enthroned ruler; and Mary as the empress. Correspondingly, worship was marked by a greater sense of awe. Prof. Wright notes that, in this period, "Growing demand for continence and increasing emphasis on the remote divinity of Christ" (led to) less frequent communion by the laity. The medieval Eucharist was regarded less as a communion of the faithful and more as a propitiatory sacrifice effected by the priests. The laity "heard mass" rather than "made their communion." When the laity did partake, which was rare, they received the bread but not the wine. The attitude toward the Eucharist was one of reverent awe rather than participatory celebration. This devotional approach to the Eucharist was linked, not logically but by historical association, with the doctrine of transubstantiation which purported to explain the mystery of bread and wine becoming the Body and Blood of Christ.

After the Carolingian reforms (twelfth century), there was an even greater emphasis on the nature of the eucharistic presence within the elements, as distinguished from the eucharistic presence within the whole assembly. While differences of interpretation were certainly possible, it could well appear to the medieval worshiper that Christ was sacrificed anew in each mass to propitiate God to forgive the sins of contemporary Christians, or even to forgive sins of the dead for which they had been consigned to Purgatory. Medieval liturgy was marked by an increase of "private" masses to honor saints whose relics were kept in the altars; and the practice of "votive masses" offered for individual needs multiplied. The mass became more an occasion for private devotions. Much of the service was now said inaudibly or even silently by the priest.[9]

The Protestant reformers vehemently rejected the medieval doctrine of the Eucharist that was captured in the phrase "the sacrifices of masses." There was no consensus among the Protestant reformers themselves as to the proper theological interpretation of the eucharistic mystery. There was a clear emphasis, however, on reviving the images of memorial and communion of the faithful.

The early Anglican perspective on the Eucharist is not subject to a simple statement. Cranmer's own doctrine of the Eucharist evolved, and the Church's doctrine remained in some flux after Cranmer.[10] There were many perspectives on the Eucharist competing to become the established doctrine of the Church of England. The Thirty-Nine Articles, adopted by the Church of England in 1563, became the most authoritative, if not altogether clear or comprehensive, statement of the Anglican view, holding:

> *The Supper of the Lord is not only a sign of the love that Christians ought to have among themselves one to another; but rather it is a Sacrament of our Redemption by Christ's death: insomuch that to such as rightly, worthily, and with faith, receive the same, the Bread which we break is a partaking of the Body of Christ; and likewise the Cup of Blessing is a partaking of the Blood of Christ. Transubstantiation (or the change of the substance of Bread and Wine) in the Supper of the Lord, cannot be proved by Holy Writ; but is repugnant to the plain words of Scripture, overthroweth the nature of a Sacrament, and hath given occasion to many superstitions. . . . And the mean whereby the Body of Christ is received and eaten in the Supper, is Faith.*[11]

The principal dispute that the Church had to resolve was between those persuaded by Zwingli that the Eucharist is fundamentally a memorial versus those who adhered to the Lutheran view which emphasized the real presence of Christ and the imparting of grace.

Chapter Seven contains the efforts of Anglican writers to build upon the framework of the Thirty-Nine Articles in order to achieve a persuasive, adequate resolution of this dispute. The excerpts in Chapter Seven begin with Jewel writing during the early phase of Anglican defense of the Prayer Book rite against criticisms from all competing parties. The readings continue as the Church of England struggled toward an understanding of the Eucharist definitive enough to ensure orthodox faith and yet not too restrictive or dogmatic regarding points on which faithful Christians might differ.

B. Major Themes

1. *Frequent Communion.* The most patent concern of the writers included in this chapter is the admonition to partake of the Eucharist frequently. To the modern reader this may seem to be an admonition directed against apathy and laxity. That, however, is not really the problem which these writers are addressing. The barrier that precluded the medieval laity from frequent participation in the Eucharist was a scrupulous concern for "worthiness" to receive the sacrament.

A recent confession, performed penance, and declaration of absolution were required in order to render the would-be communicant fit to approach the altar. Thus, when the Fourth Lateran Council in 1215 prescribed that Christian laity should receive the consecrated bread once each year, the purpose was to set a minimum standard at a higher level (more frequent participation) than was commonly observed. This is not to imply that the medieval Christian shirked church attendance. The medieval Christian frequently "heard mass," and practiced private devotions in the presence of the awesome mystery of the mass. However, a number of the Protestant reformers were committed to restoring "frequent communion" to Christian worship. That concern is reflected in Chapter Seven, beginning with Jewel's *Homily* urging Christians to participate, not merely observe, and his *Apology,* recommending that we often receive the sacrament in order to renew the remembrance daily. Sutton, Hammond, Nelson, and Seabury particularly emphasize the propriety of frequent communion.

The Companion Or Spiritual Guide At The Altar regards frequent communion as a "duty," and *The Companion To The Altar, 1826* considers a refusal to participate to constitute "guilt" of ingratitude and contempt. Hobart warns of the "danger" and "guilt" of refusing to receive the sacrament. This is a strong articulation of the demand for frequent communion, but it must be understood as the antidote to the long-standing concern to avoid receiving communion lest one receive unworthily. *The Companion . . .* describes scru-

ples and groundless fears that stand in the way of communion as
inspired by the devil.

2. *Worthy Reception.* Even so, Anglican writers could not disregard
the notion that one must meet certain standards in order to be worthy
to receive the sacrament. Far from it. Anglicanism has always expressed a particular concern for moral life and spiritual growth.
These concerns are related to worthiness. (The strongest expression
of Anglican concern for worthy reception actually appears in Chapter
Nine, p.390.) Yet Anglicans sought to articulate the standard of worthiness in such a way that it would foster positive spiritual practice
without creating an impediment to communion.

Jewel's *Homily* sets out the following elements of worthiness: (a)
a correct understanding of the sacrament; (b) a sure faith; and (c)
newness of life to "succeed" the receiving. This *Homily* is extremely
enlightening as to the early Anglican doctrine of the Eucharist. The
requirement of sure faith comports with the doctrine that the Body
and Blood are received only by virtue of the faith of the communicant—in contrast to a purely objective presence of Christ in the bread
and wine which could be received regardless of the communicant's
faith. Jewell holds that the presence is real, and has an objective
aspect, but may be received only subjectively though faith.[12] Thus
faith is necessary by virtue of the nature of the sacrament itself. The
student should attend closely to the phrasing of Jewel's third element
of worthy reception. "Newness of life" reflects the characteristic Anglican concern for moral religion, but what is the significance of
Jewell's statement that the "newness of life" is to "succeed"—not
precede—the receiving? Is this intended to suggest that a commitment to future righteousness, rather than past purity, is the criterion
for worthy reception?

Sutton and Secker both stress that it is the sacrament that sancti-
fies and cleanses the communicant; so purity is to be achieved in and
through communion, not prior to communion as a prerequisite to
reception. Secker urges that the communicant make himself or herself worthy, paradoxically, by acknowledging unworthiness.

Cosin's prerequisite to worthy reception is belief in the real presence. *The Companion To The Altar, 1815* requires belief upon a rational and full conviction, perhaps reflecting the earlier (late seventeenth century) theology of John Locke, whose *Reasonableness Of Christianity* articulated the essence of Christian faith as a reasonable assent to the credal proposition that Jesus is the Christ and our savior. *The Companion To The Altar, 1826* presents more spiritual/moral prerequisites to worthy reception, as distinguished from the intellectual assent that was predominant in the *1815 Companion.* The *1826 Companion* requires that the communicant must first forgive those against whom he or she has a grievance, and that examination, repentence, and prayer should precede reception. *The New Week's Preparation For Receiving Of The Lord's Supper* and *The 1826 Companion To The Altar* both prescribe the giving of money according to one's ability, and particularly the giving of alms, as requisite to a worthy communion. This may be regarded cynically, but it may also be understood in terms of the nature of the communion itself as a sacrifice of self, represented by the oblation of one's wealth, and as a union with humanity, represented by the sharing of wealth.

In addition to the foregoing direct or indirect references to worthiness, many of the excerpts in Chapter Seven prescribe specific devotions and subjective pieties to be practiced before, during, and after reception. These prescriptions are not to be equated with prerequisites to worthy reception, but they are not unrelated either. To the extent that legalistic scruples had given way as criteria for worthy reception, those scruples tended to be replaced by subjective pieties oriented toward sincere repentence. This may reflect a certain interiority, a concern for the subjective intent, particularly the penitential intent, characteristic of Anglican Spirituality at that time.

3. *The Nature And Effect Of The Eucharist.* A third important theme addressed by the authors in Chapter Seven is the nature and effect of the Eucharist. As noted above, the Church of England rejected both the Roman Catholic doctrine of transubstantiation (which was subject to various interpretations) and the Zwinglian doctrine. Inextricably linked to this metaphysical dispute is the question of the spiritual efficacy of the Eucharist: What is the value or effect of the

Eucharist? This question also relates to the issue of whether reception of the sacrament is as important as claimed by those who see the Eucharist primarily as a communion; or whether the real importance is that the Mass be celebrated as contended by those who understood the Eucharist primarily as a propitiatory sacrifice.

The excerpts included in Chapter Seven do not always purport to include a comprehensive statement of the author's view of the nature and spiritual effect of the Eucharist. The excerpts, however, give some significant insight into each author's eucharistic theology. As the writer closest to the events of the Reformation, it is not surprising that Jewel is the theologican most concerned to distinguish the Anglican doctrine from that of the Roman Church. He stresses that the Eucharist must be understood as a memorial and not a sacrifice, as a communion and not a private eating. His perspective is closer to the teachings of the early reformers than are the views of other writers anthologized in this chapter.

As Hooker's theology was more oriented toward a progressive participation in the divine nature, he stressed the value of the Eucharist as an imparting of grace to sustain the spiritual life and grace to enable growth in holiness. Thus Hooker's doctrine sees the Eucharist as a continuation of that process of sanctification initiated in Baptism, rather than a rite of justification, as he found justification to be effected in election that occurred even prior to Baptism. Nelson similarly viewed the Eucharist as an effective (not merely symbolic) means of growing in grace. Johnson regarded eucharistic celebration as a teacher of holiness and also as a seal of our pardon already received.

Cosin and Seabury focus on the sense in which Christ is really present in the Eucharist. Each denies the doctrine of transubstantiation, but asserts a real sacramental presence. Cosin speaks of mystic presence. Seabury speaks of the elements as becoming the Body and Blood in signification and mystery. Comber writes in a similar vein. He contends that God makes the bread and wine to be the Body and Blood, implicitly downplaying, without expressly denying, the importance of ritual formulas and the sacerdotal authority of priests to effect the change. Communicants are not to question how God effects the change, but to receive the elements in faith that they are to us the

Body and Blood of Christ. Thus Comber agrees that the Eucharist is essentially mysterious, and relates acceptance of this mystery to the doctrine found in the Thirty-Nine Articles to the effect that the real presence is received only by means of faith.

The Whole Duty Of Man and Patrick, writing in *Mensa Mystica,* stress the view of the Eucharist as a covenant renewal ceremony, perhaps reminiscent of the regular covenant renewal ceremonies of Old Testament Judaism. This image should be regarded in light of the covenant theology of Baptism presented in *The Whole Duty Of Man.* Patrick, however, goes on to state additional dimensions of the Eucharist, as a means of our nearer union with Christ and with each other. Likewise, *The Companion Or Spiritual Guide* characterized the Eucharist as a bond of union among Christians made one with Christ. This devotional text also taught that the Eucharist was a visible sign or pledge of inward and spiritual grace.

Taylor speaks of sacrifice in terms that may not be inconsistent with Jewel's doctrine, but Jewel probably would have felt that Taylor's language was capable of being construed as too close to Rome for comfort. Taylor began with the image, drawn from Hebrews, of Christ offering a perpetual sacrifice in Heaven. The celebration of the Eucharist represents Christ's death and commemorates his perpetual sacrifice. This is still a memorial doctrine of the Eucharist, but it differs from the Zwinglians in that it emphasizes the commemoration, not only of the historic event but of the perpetual sacrifice now occurring.

Taylor's insistence on a doctrine of eucharistic sacrifice may be understood in light of the fact that, in his day, the Prayer Book tradition was threatened by Puritan Parliamentarians, rather than Roman sympathizers. Taylor's eucharistic theology, however, is regarded by many as "receptionist" or emphasizing the faith of the communicant rather than the objectivity of the real presence of Christ in the elements. (See the biographical note on Taylor in the Appendix. Also see Taylor's view of the subjective experience of the communicant in section four of this chapter.) So his use of sacrificial imagery does not constitute a Roman eucharistic theology.

Brevint was not so concerned to deny that the Eucharist was a sacrifice as to deny that it was a "bare image or remembrance." He held the Eucharist to be a memorial, but also a communication of real and present graces, and a pledge of graces and glories to come. Brevint describes the Eucharist explicitly as a sacrifice. (Notwithstanding, Brevint places a strong emphasis in his eucharistic theology on denying transubstantiation and differentiating the Anglican doctrine from that of Rome. See the Biographical note on Brevint in the Appendix.) Secker emphasized the image of the Eucharist as a real sacrifice of ourselves, body and soul. To Patrick, the Eucharist was a representative sacrifice of Christ, and a real sacrifice of ourselves.

As the Reformation receded into the past, Anglicans increasingly felt free to use sacrificial language in connection with the Eucharist. They usually remained cautious, however, not to imply that the celebrations constituted new propitiatory sacrifices of Christ made present by transubstantiation.[13]

The *1815 Companion To The Altar,* consistent with its Lockean theology, regards the Eucharist as a profession of belief. Henshaw's theology appears to be somewhat related to that of the *1815 Companion* in his focus on the intellectual dimension of religion, but also related to the covenant theology of *The Whole Duty Of Man,* seeing the Eucharist as a means of instruction as to graces and duties.

Patrick, who had seen covenant renewal, union with Christ, communion of the faithful in the Eucharist, a representative sacrifice of Christ, and an actual sacrifice of the communicants, also describes the Eucharist using the metaphor of a feast. This is the Chapter Seven excerpt that comes closest to recognizing the image of the Eucharist as a foretaste of the messianic banquet of Heaven.

It is somewhat remarkable that Hammond, writing in 1654, should present a multidimensional image of the Eucharist, most similar to the modern articulations of Underhill and the World Council of Churches Statement on *Baptism, Eucharist, and Ministry.* He saw in the rite an instrument of great virtue to promote piety, a commemoration, a sacrifice (contrast Jewel) albeit a sacrifice of the self rather than a new sacrifice of Christ. Further, Hammond viewed the Eucharist as a means of communicating graces both of pardon and of strength, a making of a covenant, and a token of the love of believers for each other.

4. *Posture And Piety.* In a number of the excerpts, including *The Companion Or Spiritual Guide,* Secker, Hobart, and Coleridge reiterate the importance of kneeling at appropriate times during the celebration of the Eucharist. Likewise in a number of the excerpts, particularly *The Whole Duty Of Man* or Beveridge's *The Companion Or Spiritual Guide,* Hobart, Patrick and Henshaw emphasize the feelings that are appropriate for the communicant to stir up as a devotional practice. In contrast, Taylor wants to assure communicants that the absence of expected feelings or subjective experiences can have many causes, and that we should not condemn ourselves for not feeling what we think we are supposed to feel. His conception of the spiritual value of eucharistic celebration is more objective, less concerned with the vicissitudes of human emotion.

The concerns for kneeling and feeling are linked here because of an implicit connection between posture and subjective piety in the authors' writings. The preference for the kneeling posture stands in contrast to the Anglican concern for conformity to the practices of the early church. According to Professor Wright, the evidence suggests that kneeling was the prayer posture of early Christians only for private and penitential prayer. For public prayer, the early Christians stood, facing East, with their hands spread outward and upward (orans position). In fact, Canon 20 of the Council of Nicea (325) prohibited kneeling on Sundays or on any day during Easter Season, because those times were occasions for praise and joy rather than penitential prayer.[14] Many Anglicans today still practice kneeling as prescribed by the writers in Chapter Seven. Others have been influenced by the practices of the early church to the extent of standing at portions of the Eucharist at which others kneel.

5. *Union With Heavenly Prayers.* Sparrow notes that we sing the *Gloria In Excelsis*—the angelic hymn sung at Christ's birth—as he becomes one with us again in the Sacrament. Taylor relates the eucharistic celebration to the ongoing sacrifice offered by Christ in Heaven.

Patrick sees the Eucharist as a foretaste of the Heavenly banquet. Comber, Hobart, and Henshaw reiterate that the singing of the *Sanctus* unites our earthly voices with the heavenly choir in praise of God. These excerpts illuminate the image of the Eucharist as a present, earthly participation in the spiritual life consummated in the Heavenly Banquet and worship of saints and angels.

C. For Discussion

1. Articulate your own understanding of the Eucharist. Does it include elements of sacrifice? If so, who is sacrificing what to whom? Do you see it primarily as a real and present sacrifice, the commemoration of a sacrifice that occurred long ago, or a representation of an ongoing spiritual sacrifice?

As part of this question, carefully read the eucharistic prayers of the Prayer Book. Note the words spoken after the fraction. Do the language and sequence of actions have any significance for your doctrine of the Eucharist? What images of the Eucharist are suggested by the prayers of Thanksgiving on pp.339 and 365 of the American *Book Of Common Prayer?* After considering your answers to these questions, read the Catechism questions and answers on pp.859–860 of *The Book of Common Prayer.*

2. Read the postcommunion prayer on p.482 of *The Book of Common Prayer.* What images of the Eucharist are most clearly expressed in this prayer? What images are most clearly expressed in the postcommunion prayer on p.339? Why do you think we emphasize different images of the Eucharist in these different rites? Are we being inconsistent?

3. What is your understanding of *anamnesis?* Is it different from a "bare remembrance" (using Brevint's phrase)?

4. Under what circumstances, should a person abstain from receiving the sacrament? Should a person who knows himself or herself to be guilty of a serious sin refuse to receive? Suppose the person acknowledges the guilt, but is not sorry for the sin and does not intend to change his or her behavior?

Should a baptized Christian who denies the real presence of Christ receive? What about a baptized person who no longer acknowledges Jesus as the Christ? What if he or she is merely unsure? What about a baptized Christian who has renounced his or her faith to join another religion—should they first reaffirm their Baptismal Vows before participating in the Eucharist?

What do your answers to these questions say about your doctrine of the Eucharist, and how does your belief about the nature of the Eucharist guide your answers to these questions?

5. Read the Eucharistic prayers on pp.336 and 337 of the American *Book Of Common Prayer.* What do these prayers suggest about the doctrine of worthiness to receive the sacrament? Compare them to the various attitudes toward worthiness presented in Chapter Seven. After you have considered your answers to these questions, read the first Catechism question and answer on p.860 of *The Book of Common Prayer.*

6. Some of the writers regarded subjective experiences and feelings as essential elements of eucharistic piety. Taylor downplayed the significance of such subjective experiences. What is the importance of subjective feelings in the Eucharist? Is there value in focusing the mind and emotions so as to order them toward an affective experience of union with Christ and humanity?

7. Read I Corinthians 11:23–25; Matthew 26:26–29; Mark 14:22–25; Luke 22:14–20; John 6:51–58; Romans 8:34; 12:1; Hebrews 7:25; I Peter 2:5. What do these passages tell you about the New Testament authors' understandings of the Eucharist? Are they consistent with each other? Are they consistent with the views expressed in Chapter Seven? What doctrine of the Eucharist is expressed by the illustration on p.242 of *Prayer Book Spirituality?*

8. *Baptism, Eucharist, and Ministry* (citing Matthew 5:23f; I Corinthians 11:20–22; Galations 3:28) states:

The Eucharist embraces all aspects of life. . . . The eucharistic celebration demands reconciliation and sharing among all those regarded as brothers and sisters in the one family of God and is a constant challenge in the search for appropriate relationships in social, economic and political life. . . .

What do you see as the relationship between the Eucharist and social justice? Can one worthily participate in the Eucharist, as we understand it today, without undertaking some commitment to work for social justice?

CHAPTER EIGHT:

Marriage

A. Historical Context

The pedagogical problem presented by Chapter Eight is, in some sense, the opposite of that presented by Chapter Seven. This chapter makes no attempt to present any treatment of Anglican reflections on marriage since the nineteenth century, but rather focuses on the initial attempts of early Anglicanism to articulate a doctrine of marriage in the wake of confusion left by the Protestant Reformation. The pedagogical issue is whether to limit the study to the issues directly presented, or to use this chapter as a jumping-off place for a more extensive inquiry into the nature of marriage and more recent Anglican considerations of marriage.

First we need to clarify the immediate context of the three excerpts presented in Chapter Eight. The Protestant Reformation had not, by any means, attacked the institution of marriage. Indeed, the rejection of clerical celibacy may be regarded as affording to marriage a higher esteem than it had once received. The theological issue that arose around marriage was whether it was sacramental. The Protestant reformers ardently insisted that there were two sacraments and no more. The only sacraments acknowledged by the Protestants were Baptism and The Lord's Supper. This stand was taken against the Roman doctrine that there were seven sacraments, including marriage.

It might well be conjectured that the Protestant reformers were not genuinely concerned to deprive marriage of sacramental status. The real objects of their concern were ordination (which overly exalted the status of the clergy), confession (which granted the clergy too much power over salvation and which undermined salvation by faith alone), and confirmation (which detracted from Baptism). The Protestants challenged these "pseudosacraments" on the grounds that nothing could be deemed a sacrament that was not salvific and clearly instituted by God as shown by Scripture. This shot, fired at the previously listed sacraments, felled marriage as well. In this way, the Protestants, though not wishing to denigrate marriage, denied it sacramental status. The result was a somewhat confused status of marriage. The Anglican position was, predictably, even more ambiguous, as the early Anglicans sought to adopt the Protestant standard of "two sacraments," and yet preserve for marriage all the sacramental attributes that had historically been claimed for it.

The broader historical context raises issues of such complexity and depth as the assimilation of the Church into patriarchal society, the influence of gnosticism and Neo-Platonism on Christian attitudes toward sex, the impact of the tenth-century Cluniac reforms on clerical marriage, the medieval discovery of romantic love, and a host of social, legal, economic, and theological developments. The class may well wish to explore some aspects of this context in more depth. However, *Study Guide* will address only one general point concerning the broader context of these writings: the goods or moral values which had historically been held to be served by Christian marriage.

According to Professor Philip Turner, the Christian tradition has recognized four such goods: (a) unity or fellowship; (b) procreation; (c) a remedy for, or means of avoiding, sin; and (d) a school of charity in that the married life teaches us the necessity of moral virtues such as forgiveness, patience, and cooperation.[1] Students wishing to learn more about the liturgies and doctrines of Christian marriage over the centuries may wish to consult Stephenson's *Nuptial Blessing: A Study Of Christian Marriage Rites.*[2]

It would be well worthwhile for the class to bring the doctrines espoused in Chapter Eight into the light of a contemporary Anglican understanding of Christian marriage. This could be done readily by reading the Associated Parishes pamphlet "The Celebration And Blessing Of A Marriage: A Liturgical And Pastoral Commentary."[3] It is also helpful to read Mitchell's account of the modern practice to see how some of the sexism apparent in the excerpts in Chapter Eight has been redressed.[4] If the class wishes to consider the relationship between the marriage rite and contemporary relationships between the sexes, they will find a provocative set of essays in Turner's *Men & Women.* [5]

B. Major Themes

The first major theme presented is the holiness of matrimony. The issue is raised, of course, by the "two sacraments doctrine." The *Second Book Of Homilies* claims for marriage that it is "instituted of God." Hooker notes that it is a "holy bond," and that it is appropriate to celebrate marriage in the context of celebrating the sacrament of the Eucharist. These writers are stressing that, although the Church of England had rejected the Roman claim that marriage is a sacrament of the same order as Baptism, it is not a merely civil institution either; nor is it a mere concession to the weakness of carnal nature. Marriage is indeed a positive good grounded in the divine will. This assertion is not sufficient to claim sacramental status for marriage, but it does reject part of the Protestant objection to such sacramental status, in that it claims that marriage is divinely instituted.

Comber is less obvious in his claims for marriage in this regard but, if one reads him in the historical context, he may be understood as asserting an even stronger claim for a somewhat sacramental quality to the status of marriage. He cites Ephesians 5:32 to the effect that "In the New Testament, (marriage) is made the Symbol of an excellent Mystery, viz., of the Union between Christ and his Church . . ." To call marriage a symbol of a salvific mystery is very close to claiming that it is a sacrament, and to cite New Testament authority for this symbolic relationship is to challenge another of the Protestant grounds for denying sacramental status to marriage. Moreover, Comber is echoing Bernard of Clairvaux and other medieval theologians who understood marriage as a sacrament.

The *Book of Homilies* excerpt deals at some length with the function of marriage as a means to avoid sin, one of the traditional goods of marriage. It is noteworthy, however, that the author does not characterize this aspect of marriage so much as a concession to carnal human nature, but rather as a means of grace to avoid sin—again recalling the sacramental quality of marriage. Moreover, the author links this "avoidance of sin" to the role of marriage as a "school of charity" as the partners are required to "knit their minds together and not be dissevered by any division of discord." The union can be preserved only by frequent invoking of the Holy Spirit. Again, this invocation of the Holy Spirit is reminiscent of the invocation of the Spirit in Baptism and the Eucharist, and so reflects an essentially sacramental concept of marriage in that the Holy Spirit is invoked for a salvific purpose. It is important to note, however, who does the invoking of the Holy Spirit. It is not the priest, but the husband and wife themselves who are regarded as the true ministers in the marriage.

Another theme that must be addressed is the sexism of the commentaries anthologized in Chapter Eight. Given the patriarchal structure of sixteenth-century England, it is not surprising to find that both the *Book Of Homilies* and Hooker assert the inferiority of women. In fact, if the reader is offended by the excerpts included in Chapter Eight, the reader would be appropriately livid at those *Book of Homilies* comments on marriage that the editor chose to omit from this anthology. Those passages were deleted not to conceal the sexism of the time, but rather because *Prayer Book Spirituality* is intended to serve as a devotional companion to the Prayer Book, and those passages are inappropriate for that purpose. A study group, however, might find it worthwhile to review the entire homily on marriage in order to reflect on the extent of sexism then prevailing.

C. For Discussion

1. What theological attitude toward human sexuality is reflected in these three writings on Christian marriage?

2. A civil marriage is a contract between two parties, but a Prayer Book marriage involves public vows in the Church before God. What difference does this make in terms of the grounds necessary for divorce? If a vow is broken without sufficient grounds, what should be the implications of that action for the person's relationship with

the Church? Is it different from violating some aspect of the Baptismal Covenant? The Church has often treated divorced persons as excommunicate, but has less frequently denied the sacrament to those who have failed to "strive for justice and peace among all people."

3. The Associated Parishes pamphlet "The Celebration And Blessing Of A Marriage" states:

> . . . all of the liturgical actions of the Church have been sentimentalized and none more so than the rite of marriage. The liturgy of marriage has been trivialized by music, decorations, and ceremonies which seek to build a "mood" rather than to express the reality of marriage between persons who are baptized into Jesus Christ dying and rising. This "mood" seeks to perpetuate the myth that being "in love" is a permanent and lasting experience, and that "love" will overcome all adversity.

Is this a valid criticism? What should the marriage rite express? What is the Christian attitude toward being "in love"?

4. The *Book Of Homilies* stresses the importance of ongoing prayer in the life of a marriage. How can this prayer be practiced in the context of married life? How can the Church foster such prayer practice?

CHAPTER NINE

The Reconciliation of a Penitent

A. Historical Context

There is a delicate irony in the history of confession and absolution in English Christianity. The Chapter Nine excerpts were written at a sort of midpoint in that history in the wake of the Protestant Reformation. Yet to focus exclusively on controversy over this rite in the Protestant Reformation would miss both the subtlety and the irony of the Rite of Reconciliation's role in Anglican Spirituality.

The story really begins during the period after the fall of the Roman Empire, when the Church in Britain was separated from the Church in Rome, and differing customs prevailed in the two churches. The Church in Britain during this period is known to historians as the Celtic Church as the Celts were still dominant in Britain at that time. It was only after Pope Gregory I sent Augustine of Canterbury as a missionary to England that the full integration of the British Church with the rest of Christendom began. It took some time to reconcile the different religious practices of Britain and Rome.

The irony derives from the fact that frequent personal confession, the practice so abhorred by the Protestant Reformers, was the practice of the Celtic Church—not that of Rome. This was the one significant area in which Rome adapted its practices to those of Britain (although probably not for the purpose of accommodating the British), while in all other regards the British practices gave way to the Roman after the Council of Whitby in 664.

Prior to Gregory I, Rome had used this rite only in cases of serious sin, sometimes reserving it to cases in which excommunication had been imposed. Moreover, prior to Gregory, absolution could be granted only once in the sinner's lifetime. The Celts, on the other hand, regarded confession as a regular aspect of Christian life and an essential part of spiritual and moral formation. Hence personal confession was practiced for minor as well as serious sins, though confession to a priest was not regarded as an essential means to obtain God's forgiveness. The sinner's confession directly to God was deemed adequate to that end. Penances had to be freely accepted and were considered offerings to God as thanksgiving for absolution already received. The early Roman practice had been essentially disciplinary, while the Celtic practice had served as a means of spiritual direction and practice. As Thornton puts it, "The whole of the Celtic system presupposes the interrelation between morals and ascetic; or it presupposes a teleological moral theology."[1]

During the later Middle Ages, the Roman penitential system had come to be based on frequent confession and absolution, as in the Celtic tradition; however, the purpose of the system remained disciplinary. Penances were judicially imposed rather than freely accepted, and absolution was conditioned upon performance of the penances. The Anglican objections to this system, which are articulated in Chapter Nine, reflect the Protestant aversion to medieval Roman penitential doctrine. Yet these Anglicans preserve personal (auricular) confession for limited cases. Without considering the context of the Celtic tradition, this may appear to be something of a muddled compromise between the Roman and Genevan positions. However, in actuality, the doctrine of reconciliation that runs through Chapter Nine is a harkening back to the Celtic approach of regarding reconciliation as a spiritual practice rather than a disciplinary system. Nonetheless, the association with the Roman penitential tradition caused many to regard the rite suspiciously until modern times.

Only the most recent edition of *The Book of Common Prayer* has included the form for Reconciliation of a Penitent. Underhill has written,

> *Closely connected with this (re-opening and exploration of ancient devotional paths) is the gradual domestication of the once dreaded practice of confession,*

and increasing recognition of its religious and psychological worth. . . . These practices are no longer regarded as marks of an extreme Catholicism. They are accepted, and even recommended, by that sober Anglicanism of the centre which traces its descent from the Caroline Church. . . .[2]

For an explanation of the contemporary understanding of this rite, the student would do well to study the language of the forms in *The Book of Common Prayer* pp.447ff.; the catechetical teachings in *The Book of Common Prayer* at p.857 (the last Question and Answer) and p.861 ("What is Reconciliation of a Penitent?" and "Is God's activity limited to these rites?"); and Mitchell's commentary on reconciliation in *Praying Shapes Believing.* [3] Another excellent source is P. D. Butterfield's *How To Make Your Confession: A Primer For Members Of The Church Of England.* [4]

B. Major Themes

The first major theme in Chapter Nine is the adequacy of confessing one's sins directly to God, without the involvement of a priest, as a means to secure absolution for one's sins. The *Book Of Homilies* assaults the practice of mandatory personal confession to a priest as unreasonable, unscriptural, and unpatristic (contrary to the tradition of the early church); but the author does urge that in cases of sin which have caused animosity among the faithful, it is appropriate to confess to those from whom one is estranged. Jewel denies that the authority to bind and loose (Matthew 16:19; 18:18—the scriptural grounds traditionally relied upon to support the Roman penitential system) actually authorized such priestly power over absolution. He argued that the text referred instead to preaching. (Thorndike would later make the opposite argument.)

Hooker emphasized the primary importance of inward repentance, and held that the priestly authority to absolve sinners was exercised in the public confession and absolution, allowing only limited exceptions for private confession and absolution. Although Wake defends the practice of voluntary private confession, he emphasizes that Anglicans do not consider this practice to be necessary to salvation.

The second major theme is that personal confession, though not required, is permissible and is sometimes pastorally advisable. Hooker conceives of confession as both a disciplinary measure occasionally needed to ensure worthy reception of the Eucharist and as a pastoral assurance for those on the verge of death. *The Whole Duty* concurs with regard to the need to assure worthy reception of the Eucharist. Thorndike, Wake, and L'Estrange defend the practice more broadly to relieve a sense of guilt in any context that leads the penitent to seek absolution.

The third major theme deals with the spiritual significance of the pronouncement of absolution by the priest. Hooker, Thorndike, and Wake all regarded the pronouncement of absolution as a declaration of a forgiveness that had already occurred: God had promised to forgive all those who were truly penitent, so the priest's pronouncement was merely a sort of assurance. L'Estrange saw the pronouncement of absolution as containing three distinct parts: a prayer to God to forgive the penitent, a declaration that God has forgiven the penitent, and an authoritative absolution of the penitent by virtue of the authority of the Church.

C. For Discussion

1. The Church of England, at the time of these texts, held to the "two sacraments" standard of the Protestant Reformation. The Catechism sections referred to in the first Section above hold that Reconciliation of a Penitent is also a sacrament. How does this status as a sacrament affect the importance we attribute to the pronouncement of absolution? What do you consider to be the value of a pronouncement of absolution (in either private or public confession)?

2. *The Book Of Common Prayer* authorizes any lay person to hear confession and declare forgiveness. The right to pronounce absolution, however, is restricted to priests. In light of this fact, would you say our current understanding of absolution is more in line with L'Estrange or with Hooker, Wake, and Thorndike? How do you understand the difference between a declaration of forgiveness and a pronouncement of absolution?

3. In Chapter Four we reflected on the role of contrition or penitence in a healthy spirituality, considering such sources as Ulanov's *Primary Speech* and Booty's "Contrition In Anglican Spirituality." How do the themes from those sources apply to the rite of Reconciliation of a Penitent? Consider the element of faith, as described in the *Book Of Homilies* excerpt in Chapter Nine. How does faith relate to the distinction between constructive contrition and morbid guilt?

4. The Ignatian Spirituality of Jesuits calls for a regular examination of conscience and repentance. What is the value of regular self-examination for spiritual growth?

5. Hooker regarded confession and absolution to some extent as a disciplinary measure for the moral guidance of the laity by the clergy. Is this approach more consistent with the Roman or the Celtic tradition? Hooker wrote in the social context of an established church that shared with the secular government the responsibility for public order. In a society in which Church and State are substantially separated, is the Church's disciplinary responsibility different?

6. There are two dominant styles for the rite of Reconciliation. One is quite formal, often with the identity of the penitent concealed from the priest. The other is more informal and involves more dialogue and pastoral counseling. What do you see as the advantages and disadvantages of each approach?

CHAPTER TEN:

Ministration to the Sick

A. Historical Context.

The character of this rite, then known as Visitation To The Sick, is well captured by the illustration at the beginning of Chapter Ten. It is quite apparent that no one in this picture is expecting the sick woman to recover. The basic tenor of the rite is aptly demonstrated by Sparrow's admonition to the visiting priest to see that the sick person has settled his estate "for the discharging of his own conscience, and the quietness of his executors." In brief, this ministration was chiefly regarded as last rites. It is helpful to consider (a) how the rite came to be so regarded, and (b) the continuing historical developments subsequent to the writings included in this chapter.

The most accessible source on the history of Christian ministration to the sick is Morton T. Kelsey's *Psychology, Medicine, and Christian Healing.* [1] Kelsey begins with the Scriptural accounts of healings by Jesus and his disciples and of continuing healing ministries during the Apostolic Age. Healing continued to be a ministry in the church of the patristic era as evidenced in the lives and works of such early Christians as St. Basil, Gregory of Nazianzus, John Chrysostom, and Hyppolytus. St. Augustine once wrote that the gift of healing should not be expected to continue; however, he later reversed his position, and attested to "nearly seventy (healing) miracles" in his diocese.

At least by the fifth century, the healing ministry was largely focused on the sacrament of unction or anointing with oil, which could be administered by clergy or laity. For a complex set of reasons, however, none of which related to advances in science, illness came to be regarded as a scourge of God to punish sin, and healing fell into disfavor. Earthly life was seen as a sordid occasion of trial; and death as a welcome escape. Hence, by the ninth century, the Western church was beginning to transform unction for healing into unction as preparation for death. (Miraculous healings remained a part of medieval faith, but they came to be associated with relics and saints rather than the sacraments of the Church.) The Scholastic Theology of the later Middle Ages also took a dim view of healing sacraments, leaving unction to be the last step in the penitential system.

The Protestant Reformers agreed that the ministry of the Church should be addressed more to preparation for the next life than to foster health in this one. There was no room at all for unction in their system, as they rejected the penitential doctrines that had come to define unction for the Roman Church. As for England, Kelsey notes:

> *In England . . . sickness came to be viewed as a particular punishment given by God for our good. There was probably no worse place in the Christian world to be sick and destitute than in England in the seventeenth and eighteenth centuries. The monasteries, which had provided healing and also physical care for the sick and the destitute . . . were wiped out entirely. . . . (I)n 1552 anointing was dropped from the Order for Visitation, leaving English Christians with the idea firmly planted that even their peccadilloes would bring on gout, if not something worse.'*[2]

This "dressing of a soul for a funeral" was the pastoral principle that guided the excerpts in Chapter Ten, but that principle does not define modern practice. Mitchell writes:

> *If we are looking for changes in theology in the Book Of Common Prayer 1979, we will do well to look at the Ministration to the Sick. It replaces the Visitation of the Sick, the least used and least useable service in the 1928 Prayer Book. Earlier forms based on medieval models accurately reflected the state of medical science in the sixteenth century and did not seriously consider the possibility that the sick person might recover. They tended to pray for grace to accept sickness patiently and die well. The anointing of the sick came to be popularly called "last rites," and it was administered*

only to those in danger of death. The rites also tended to treat sickness as a punishment for sin.[3]

Mitchell goes on to state that the theological thrust of the 1979 rite is, precisely, healing. Moreover, the change cannot be tied exclusively to the charismatic movement in the Episcopal Church that arose in the 1960s, as the reaction against the "last rites" approach began with the addition of genuine healing prayers in the 1928 Prayer Book.[4] One might surmise that this new hope for healing had its roots in the more life-affirming, incarnation-centered modern theologies exemplified by Maurice, Gore, and Temple, which in turn drew upon the eighteenth-century writings of Joseph Butler. Mitchell notes, however, that the 1979 Prayer Book does include additional provisions for Ministration at the time of death.

B. Major Themes

The first major theme is that of pastoral guidance or spiritual direction aimed at preparation for the heavenly life. Taylor emphasizes the continuity between this pastoral guidance and the pastoring of the soul thoughout life. Sparrow presents a similar approach emphasizing the need for self-examination on one's deathbed. It is important to recognize the distinction between these "last rites" and the Roman tradition. The action here is pastoral rather than sacramental in character, and relies upon earnest exortation by the minister rather than any sacramental efficacy of his words or deeds.

Second, notwithstanding the overwhelming emphasis upon preparation for death, Taylor recommends that the minister be called upon in times of illnesses that are not fatal. He regards illness as a time in which one is particularly aware of creatureliness and therefore may be open to pastoral initiative for growth in the faith.

Third, Comber emphasizes the moral obligation, not only of the clergy but of all Christians, to visit the sick and needy to give them comfort. While the approach in this period may have taken a less optimistic view of the role of grace in earthly life than we hold today, it is important to remember that the two purposes of the classical Visitation to the Sick were beneficent: the reconciliation of the dying

Christian to God and other people; and the offering of comfort and consolation to our fellow mortals.

C. For Discussion

1. Since the publication of Elizabeth Kubler-Ross's *On Death And Dying*[5] and the growth of the hospice movement, we have become particularly aware of the potential for spiritual growth and resolution during a final illness. What implications does this have for ministry to the dying? Do these insights suggest that some form of healing may occur even though the person dies? You may wish to read Linn, Linn, and Linn *Healing The Dying* to gain perspective on this question.[6] Now consider the pastoral practices described in Chapter Ten in light of the Kubler-Ross model of dying. What is the value of facilitating reconciliation before death?

2. Sometimes people experience a recovery from their physical illness after prayers for healing; sometimes they do not. In the latter event, some people blame the failure to cure the illness on the inadequate faith of the sick person or of the people who prayed. Is this a valid theological perspective on healing? Why or why not? What other reasons might prevent a physical recovery? Does the lack of a physical recovery necessarily mean that the prayers have failed? For a Catholic charismatic perspective, see MacNutt, *Healing.*[7]

3. Serious illnesses and impending death create pastoral needs not only in the person who is ill, but also in family, friends, and health-care professionals. Should the rite for the sick also attempt to address these needs in some way? If so, what would you recommend?

4. The tension between praying for healing and preparation for dying may reflect the difficulty in finding a Christian affirmation of life that also affirms the grace of God in the midst of death. How was this conflict reconciled in each of the three excerpts in Chapter Ten? How is it reconciled in our modern pastoral approach and the 1979 rite?

5. The anointing with oil for healing is now regarded as a sacrament. In what sense is it a sacrament? In what other ways is healing grace imparted to the sick? What is the relationship between sacramental healing, faith healing, and medical healing?

CHAPTER ELEVEN:

The Burial of the Dead

A. Historical Context

The excerpts in this chapter reflect a view of the Christian burial rite that is still held in many parts of the Anglican Communion that strictly adhere to the 1662 Prayer Book; however, it differs in important respects from the perspective of the 1979 edition of the Prayer Book in the United States. Although these excerpts are not polemical, they strongly reflect the influence of the Protestant Reformation, and are separated from modern American practice by the intervention of the Oxford Movement (nineteenth-century Anglo-Catholic theology) and the modern liturgical reforms.

To understand the context of these excerpts, we must first consider the doctrine of purgatory that was held by the pre-Reformation Church. The doctrine underwent changes, and was understood in various ways; but the central point was that, although the ultimate fate and salvation of the soul was established at the time of death, that soul might yet be required to undergo a period of purification during which punishments would be endured as satisfaction for sins committed during life. This doctrine was well grounded in Christian antiquity, claiming the support of St. Clement of Alexandria, Origen, St. Cyril of Jerusalem, St. Ambrose, St. Augustine, and many others. During the Later Middle Ages, prayers for the dead, funeral masses (understood as propitiatory sacrifices), and pious works performed by the living on behalf of the dead were thought to be effective means to lighten the punishments and shorten the duration of purgatory so as to expedite the journey of the deceased to final union with God. The major Protestant Reformers, however, rejected the existence of purgatory.[1] Accordingly, the Protestant Churches abandoned funeral masses and prayers for the dead as superstitious.

The first doctrinal statement of the Church of England was the Ten Articles that appeared in 1536 during the moderate stage of the English Reformation. In the Ten Articles, prayers for the dead were retained but the doctrine of purgatory was omitted.[2] The 1552 edition of the Prayer Book was more distinctively Protestant, and dropped all prayers for the dead. Prayer for the dead was not reinstated until the 1928 American *Book of Common Prayer.*[3]

Mitchell offers a concise statement of the theology of these prayers:

> . . . (*The prayer at BCP:481 asks*) *for growth in knowledge and love of God. Behind the prayer lies the recognition that no one is ready at the time of death to enter into life in the nearer presence of God without substantial growth precisely in love, knowledge and service; and the prayer also recognizes that God will provide what is necessary for us to enter that state. This growth will presumably take place between death and resurrection, but Scripture does not provide enough information to do more than speculate on how this growth will happen. . . . The liturgy is vague, because we walk without knowledge but with firm faith in Christ's love and promises.*[4]

Thus the modern doctrine is not a revisit of the juridical, penitential, punitive purgatory of medieval theology. It is instead a view of death as a step in the journey of the soul toward God, and a statement of faith that God will bring us home by a path of grace.

The excerpts in Chapter Eleven are drawn from the period after 1552, when prayer for the dead ceased and before the Oxford Movement, when segments of Anglicanism became more open to some Roman practices. Thus the approach to funerals in these excerpts focuses on pastoral needs of the living and a clear evangelical proclamation of the Resurrection faith, rather than on any benefit that might be secured to the deceased by the rite. The pastoral and proclamatory dimensions of the burial rite are still present, but the rite is also perceived as an occasion to offer effective prayers for the deceased and to commend his or her soul to the care of God.

From an anthropological standpoint, students might find it interesting to compare this element of the Christian burial to the practices of Native Americans in equipping the deceased with food and supplies for a journey from the land of the living to the final blessed land hereafter; or to the Tibetan practice of ongoing guidance for the dead who are believed to be at a crucial stage in their spiritual path. Students who wish to gain a more specific grasp of contemporary pastoral and theological issues in Christian burial are encouraged to read the Associated Parishes pamphlet *The Burial Of The Dead.*[5]

B. Major Themes

The first prominent theme is faith in the resurrection of the body. Each author cites this belief. Jewel and Comber particularly emphasize belief in the physicality of the resurrection, using such terms as "our selfsame flesh" and "God will one day enquire for this Body again." The care for proper burial was itself an expression of the belief that the body would be resurrected.

The second theme is the propriety of expressing love for and honor to the deceased. This theme appears chiefly in Hooker. The third theme is the Church's loving concern for the bereaved. This theme appears in Hooker and implicitly in Sparrow's section on the bidding of the last farewell. Finally, Comber notes a concern for the posture and position of the corpse (the pointing of the feet to the East). This demonstrates characteristic Anglican attention to detail in general and bodily positions in particular as expressions of our relationship to God.

C. For Discussion

1. How literally and how physically do you interpret the doctrine of the resurrection of the body? Read St. Paul's discourse on the nature of the resurrection in I Corinthians 15:35–50. If the body which is resurrected is the "spiritual body," how should we regard the physical body of the deceased? Is the care we show in burial to be understood as a symbolic expression of love for the person and hope for the spiritual resurrection, or is it a matter of literal belief in physical resurrection? For an articulation of the doctrine of the bodily resurrection which is not only authoritative but simultaneously amusing

and profound, students should read Augustine's *City Of God,* Book XXII, chapters 12–21.[6]

2. Why do we pray for the dead? You will find the Catechism answer on p.862 of *The Book Of Common Prayer.* What do you think? Is death the end of the spiritual journey? Do prayers for the departed actually benefit the departed? Are they of any benefit to the one who prays?

3. Sparrow notes that ancient tradition supports celebrating the Eucharist at a funeral, but he does not offer a theological justification. What do you suppose would have been the point of celebrating the Eucharist at a medieval funeral? What would be the purpose in an Anglican funeral?

4. Read the rubric on p.507 of *The Book Of Common Prayer.* What are the roles of joy and grief in a Christian funeral?

CHAPTER TWELVE

Ordination

A. Historical Context

The descriptions of ordained ministry in the Chapter Twelve excerpts may strike the modern reader as stuffy, pretentious, and authoritarian. If we look, however, at the historical context in which the authors wrote, their descriptions may appear in a rather different light. Certainly much has changed in our understanding of ministry since these texts were written, but some of the issues that they address are still with us. Indeed, those issues are at the heart of conflicts that still trouble the Anglican Communion and which are at the center of many ecumenical dialogues.

The ordering of ministry in the Church has been an issue since Jesus first called the disciples and they promptly began arguing over who should be first among them.[1] In the Apostolic Age, the apostles exercised chief authority, but other ministries were also recognized, including prophets, teachers, and elders.[2]

The Pastoral Epistles, which probably reflect the practices of second-generation Christianity, speak of a different ordering of ministry, including the offices of bishop (*episcopos,* meaning overseer) and deacon (derived from *diakonia,* meaning service).[3] During the second century, this ordering of ministry assumed the form of the "threefold order"—bishops, priests, and deacons—that generally prevailed in most places for most of the Patristic Era. During the Middle Ages, the hierarchical ordering of ministry was regarded as divinely prescribed and reflective of spiritual realities. The three orders were expanded, however, to allow for other ordained liturgical functionaries. The doctrine of Apostolic Succession (a doctrine that began in the first century but was subject to varying and evolving interpretations) was widely held to mean that the validity of ordination depended on a sort of "pipeline of grace" in which Christ had laid hands on the Apostles, who laid hands on their successors, who ordained their successors, and so on up to the contemporary clergy.[4]

Many medieval clergymen were, no doubt, genuine pastors and spiritual guides to their parishioners. But the medieval theology of ordained ministry emphasized the role of the priest as one who offers sacrifices (in the Eucharist) and pronounces absolution pursuant to divine authority. The advent of private masses underscored this aspect of priesthood in the later Middle Ages.

The Protestant Reformation rejected not only the Roman penitential system but also the ordering of ministry which was so closely related to the sacrifices of masses, pronouncement of absolutions, and prescribing of penances. Once again, however, the English reformers took a middle course that was problematic both to Roman Catholics and to Puritans. The Church of England maintained the threefold order of ministry and at least purported to maintain the practice of Apostolic Succession as it had been followed in the Roman Church. Like the Reformed Churches, the Anglican ordinals emphasized that the ministerial office could not be separated from the authority and ministry of the congregation. The Thirty-Nine Articles and the Preface to the 1550 Ordinal gave equal significance to requiring ordained ministry to be authorized by the wider Church (i.e., higher Church authority), as ordination required the consent and involvement of the bishop. The first Anglican ordinals emphasized preaching as "God's instrument of salvation," and omitted any sacrificial language, yet retained the ministerial title of "priest" which the Puritans associated with the concept of sacrifice.[5]

Roman Catholics challenged the validity of Anglican ordinations, claiming defects in the chain of ordinations—the "pedigree" of Anglican clerics. Puritans took offense at the word "priest" and attacked the hierarchical authority of bishops over other ministers as unscriptural. Anglicans were therefore concerned to defend the claim that their ordained ministry was lawful and grounded in divine institution. They wanted to show that the threefold order was consonant with

Scripture and practiced by the early church, and that "priest" was derived from *"presbyter"* (meaning elder, and hence reflecting a pastoral ministry) and not from *"sacerdos"* (a term connoting cultic functions such as sacrifice).[6]

The Chapter Twelve descriptions of ordained ministry must also be understood in the context of an established church. Throughout most of the Anglican Communion, churches are voluntary associations, but that is not the context in which these authors wrote. O. C. Edwards notes:

> *In the Episcopal Church in the USA . . . parish clergy function in many ways as chaplains to the people who have voluntarily associated themselves with the local community which practices the Christian faith as this communion has received it. Their conception of their responsibility is very different from that which Church of England priests have for certainly the spiritual and to an extent the physical welfare of all who live within the bounds of their parishes.*[7]

The patronage system plays an even more important role in some of the concerns of the Chapter Twelve authors, and that system is quite alien to most modern readers, who are accustomed to priests who are called by the congregation and then proceed to actually minister to the people who called them. The patronage system worked differently, however. Each parish provided an income for a priest; but the monasteries which had founded the parishes in the Middle Ages retained the right to appoint the priest of that parish. After the monasteries were dissolved by Henry VIII, the right to appoint priests was held, in the case of some parishes, by a local squire whose ancestor had been given that right by King Henry. In other cases the King retained the right to make the appointment. In still others, the bishop made the appointment. Customarily, however, the person appointed did not actually minister to the parish. Frequently he received appointments to receive the incomes from several parishes, and then hired curates to perform his ministries.[8]

Not surprisingly, as John Webster has observed, "Anglicanism emerged in a period of generally lax ministerial practice. . . . The revival of pastoral ministry thus became a prime concern, not the least because of the need to establish a firm clerical base in the midst of competing confessions of faith."[9] This revival was accomplished, but there was a serious decline in the practice of ministry in the first half of the eighteenth century as pluralism (holding more than one clerical position) and absenteeism (living outside one's parish) became rampant. The Methodist and Evangelical movements, the Plurality Acts of 1838 and 1850, and the Oxford Movement eventually led to significant reforms in this inadequate system of clergy deployment.[10] These movements resulted in the "professionalization" of the clergy. As O. C. Edwards puts it, ". . . in the nineteenth century, clergy took the professions that were emerging at the time as their 'model and reference group.' Prior to that, the role of the clergy was that of 'an occupational appendage of gentry status.' "[11] At the time the Chapter Twelve excerpts were written, however, it remained necessary to exhort the ordained gentry to regard their ordination as a serious responsibility, rather than an occasion to receive incomes comparable to feudal rents.

Today, ecumenical dialogue, women's ordination, and the demand for recognition of meaningful lay vocations are the occasions of reexamining our beliefs about the nature and meaning of the ordained ministry. Important clarifications in our doctrine of ministry are expressed in ecumenical statements such as *God's Reign And Our Unity* (from the Anglican-Reformed Dialogue), *Ministry And Ordination* (from the Anglican-Roman Catholic Dialogue), and *The Niagra Report* (from the Anglican-Lutheran Consultation).[12]

Students would do well to consult *Baptism, Eucharist, And Ministry* for a concise statement of contemporary theology of ministry.[13] The emerging themes of these statements suggest a trend toward recognizing the threefold order of ministry, and seeing bishops as symbols of unity of the Church. Apostolic Succession is sometimes regarded as an important symbol of the unity of Christians today with the Christians of times past, but the concept of "apostolicity," as essential to valid ministry, is focused more on the continuing of the same teachings, mission, and functions that we see in the original Apostles, rather than upon the linear chain of succession or "pedigree."

B. Major Themes

The first major theme in Chapter Twelve is the nature of the authority of the ordained ministry. This theme raises issues of apostolicity and the necessity of ordination by the Bishop of the diocese rather than mere election by the parish congregation. Hooker notes that ministry is divinely instituted. The authority of the priest is derived from God, not people, so one can become a priest only when one is lawfully ordained by the Church. Ordination is possible because the Church contains the spirit of Christ, so it can convey spiritual gifts of authority. Once that spiritual power is so conferred, it cannot be voluntarily relinquished. Ordination is an act of God that mere humans cannot undo. Wake concurs with Hooker, emphasizing that ministry may be assumed only by lawful ordination.

A related theme is the sacramental quality of ordination. Puritans had rejected the sacramental quality of ordination, but Wake explicitly refers to ordination as a "particular sacrament" to distinguish it from the two general sacraments, Baptism and Eucharist, which are available to all Christians and are necessary to salvation. Hooker does not expressly call ordination a sacrament, but he does describe it in terms of an actual imparting of spiritual gifts, not a mere election or appointment to an office or function.

The third theme is the pastoral versus the sacramental or cultic function of the minister. (This may be a conflation of two themes, but separating them would obscure the issue.) Hooker raises the issue in his defense of the use of the controversial title "priest." He defends the term (albeit not too vigorously) on the grounds that "priest" has traditionally denoted a minister of the Gospel, and does not necessarily imply one who offers a sacrifice. Sparrow, on the other hand, defends the use of "priest" as meaning one who is in charge of holy things. Anglican priests, he contends, are indeed charged with such responsibility, and they do offer sacrifices of prayers, praise, and thanksgiving. Sparrow goes on to argue that the Eucharist is a "commemorative sacrifice" and that the offering of bread and wine is the priestly sacrifice of Melchizedek.

This discrepancy between Hooker and Sparrow reflects the unresolved state of early Anglican eucharistic theology and the resultant ambiguity of the early Anglican theology of ministry. The pastoral role, however, was vigorously stressed as the primary responsibility of Anglican clergy during this time. The works of Comber and Simeon are clear statements of this pastoral role. These excerpts must be understood as attempts to instill an ideal of pastoral ministry that would overcome the laxity which prevailed under the patronage system. Simeon's concern that priests should not enter the ministry for financial gain seems curious, given present-day clergy salaries; but in a day when ordination could bring several "incomes" with no ministerial responsibilities, the concern was real. Comber and Sparrow regard priests as standing spiritually *in loco parentis* to their parishioners, and having a responsibility to shepherd them through the moral maze of a sinful world. The paternalism of this model must be understood in terms of the established church mentality and the hierarchical class structure inherited from the feudal system.

C. For Discussion

1. The pressing conflict with regard to the role of clergy in the early days of Anglicanism was that of the "sacrificial priest" versus the "pastor." Is that still a problem in the church today? Which of these images predominates in your idea of the clergy?

2. A pressing conflict with regard to the role of the clergy today is that of "authoritative leader" versus "servant." Would this conflict have been possible in the class structure of seventeenth-century England? Which of these images predominates in your idea of the clergy? Which should primarily shape the actual role of the clergy? Can these roles be reconciled?

3. How would you compare and contrast the ministries of laity, deacons, priests, and bishops? The Catechism questions and answers on pp.855 and 856 of *The Book of Common Prayer* are a helpful starting point. Are the ministries of these orders entirely different?

4. The doctrine of Apostolic Succession is the most difficult issue in many ecumenical dialogues. What is the importance of this doctrine in your faith? What do you think of the reinterpretations of the doctrine in the modern ecumenical agreements?

5. The authors in Chapter Twelve stress the necessity of lawful ordination, which included not only the element of historical succession, but also the element of ordination by the church as a wider body than the local assembly. In the Episcopal Church, bishops ordain parish priests with the advice and consent of Diocesan committees and commissions. A parish cannot call a priest as its rector without the consent of the bishop. A Diocese's election of its bishop cannot be implemented without approval of the House of Bishops. How do you justify these practices? Compare these practices to the polities of the Roman Catholic Church and the Congregational Church. Why do Anglicans do these things differently?

6. Richard Hooker is regarded by many as the greatest proponent for the authority of tradition in Anglicanism, and tradition is often cited as grounds for resisting changes in the ordering of ministry. Yet Hooker wrote in opposition to the Puritans who attacked the three-fold order because ministry was not so ordered in the churches of New Testament days. Hooker wrote:

> . . . in tying the Church to the orders of the Apostles times, they tye it to a mervelous uncertaine rule . . . But then is not this their rule of such sufficiencie, that we should use it as a touchstone to try the orders of the Church by for ever. Our ende ought alwaies to bee the same, our waies and meanes thereunto not so. The glorie of God and the good of his Church was the thing which the Apostles aymed at, and therefore ought to be the marke whereat we also levell. But seeing those rites and orders may be at one time more, which at an other are lesse availeable unto that purpose: what reason is there in these thinges to urge the state of one onely age, as a patterne for all to followe?[14]

What do you see as the "touchstone" or guiding principle to control the church's ordering of its ministry in our time? What are the respective roles of Scripture, tradition, and reason?

CHAPTER THIRTEEN:

Catechetical Instruction and Preaching

A. Historical Context

The subjects of Catechetical Instruction and Preaching are an apt conclusion to this collection of writings on *Prayer Book Spirituality*. They complete what Thornton has called the "integrated ascetical system" of *The Book of Common Prayer.* In the classical age of Anglicanism, catechetical instruction and preaching assumed a distinctive role in the spiritual life of English Christians. But the nature of that role had not been at all clear at the inception of the Church of England.

In reading the excerpt from Richard Hooker, *On Preaching and Catechising,* it might be easy to misapprehend his point. When his passage is placed in context we see that Hooker is not praising preaching as we think of it, but rather is arguing that sermons are not necessary to a valid and complete worship service. The Puritans, with their strong emphasis on the expounding of Scripture for the edification of the people, insisted that the sermon should be the centerpiece of Christian worship. This focus on the sermon in mainline Protestantism is architecturally expressed by the central positioning of the pulpit in many Protestant churches even today. This is to be contrasted with the architectural expression of modern Anglican churches in which the altar is centrally placed, and the pulpit or lectern stands to the side.

The Puritans of Elizabethan England held the worship of the Church of England to be deficient because sermons were often lacking. The reason for such a dearth of sermons was not theological, but practical. The ordained clergy actually serving in parishes were quite poorly educated. Bear in mind that the actual parish clergy were curates receiving rather modest pay from absentee rectors who received the income of the parish by virtue of patronage.[1] Given the state of theological controversy, not to mention the relative subtlety of the Anglican position on a number of issues, it was not viable to have church doctrine expounded in pulpits by an untrained clergy, so most curates were not licensed to preach.

Hooker's defense, of which a part is included in Chapter Thirteen, was that the expounding of Scripture was adequately accomplished by the substantial reading of Scripture in public worship and by catechetical instruction. Notwithstanding Hooker's insistence that sermons were not essential to valid worship, his own sermons were lengthy, eloquent, and erudite. The Anglican clerics of the next century followed Hooker's example, rather than his words denigrating the importance of the sermon, and constituted the seventeenth century as a veritable "golden age of English rhetoric." The sermons of Lancelot Andrewes and John Dunne are still read as literary masterpieces. The excerpt from Herbert reflects the broad prevalence of this new emphasis on the sermon, indicating that excellent preaching was the responsibility of the country parson as well as deans of St. Paul's Cathedral such as Dunne.

In a sense, the Puritans finally carried the day in the debate over the necessity of sermons. In the Episcopal Church today, a sermon or homily is preached at any celebration of the Eucharist on a Sunday or major feast day.[2] The initial weakness of this element in Anglican worship, however, may also have had a lasting and beneficial effect. In the absence of strong sermons, catechetical instruction became more than a preconfirmation ordeal for the young. Catechetical instruction became an important, ongoing part of the Christian life. Later, when the sermon emerged as a prominent feature of Anglican worship, it took its place in relation to a foundation of catechesis.

Because of the prominence of sermons in the era of the Caroline Divines (seventeenth century), it is sometimes said that the sermon replaced the confessional for Anglicans, as the context for moral instruction. Thornton, however, regards this as a dangerous half-truth. He contends that:

Catechism, preaching, and guidance, together constituted "the ministry of the word," which becomes almost synonymous with spiritual guidance itself in the wider, empirical, Anglican sense. Neither catechism nor preaching were concerned with intellectual, or "academic," teaching, but with Christian living: it is all ascetical theology, "practical divinitie," spiritual direction.[3]

Catechetical instruction provided the basic framework for pastoral practice. Preaching, then, was intended to expound Scripture in such a way as to inspire the congregation to live out the truths learned in catechesis. Finally, one-to-one guidance (sometimes in the context of confession, but often not) personalized the application of these matters to the life of the individual Christian. These practices were linked in the single pastoral purpose, which O. C. Edwards articulates this way: ". . . the object of Anglican pastoral ministry is the sanctification of the people of God."[4]

The role of preaching and catechetical instruction need to be understood in the context of the total Prayer Book way of life. These activities must be seen in relation to Baptism, Confirmation, the Daily Office, Reconciliation, Eucharist, Ministry To The Sick, and Burial Of The Dead. These are not isolated rites or practices, but all related parts of a single spirituality of relationship with God and humanity.

B. Major Themes

The first major theme is the interrelatedness of catechizing and preaching. This appears in Hooker's actually equating "instruction" with "preaching." Herbert does not equate catechizing with preaching, since there are purposes which preaching can accomplish but catechizing cannot; Herbert, however, shows that this difference of purpose makes catechizing and preaching essential complements to each another.

The second theme is that catechetical instruction is not for the young only but is intended, according to Herbert, to be ongoing. It not only is meant to ensure minimal understanding by the "elder sort who are not well grounded," but also in order that even the learned may be prompted to "examine their grounds, renew their vows, and . . . enlarge their meditations," in Herbert's words. *The Whole Duty*

Of Man also emphasizes that adults are "not exempt" from the need for such instruction.

The third theme is that catechesis is not the responsibility of the clergy alone. Herbert and *The Whole Duty Of Man* both emphasize the duty of parents to teach their children and of masters to teach their servants. This theme reminds us of the vital importance of domestic piety in classical Anglicanism.

The fourth theme is the purpose of catechesis and preaching in contributing to the sanctification—the making holy—of the people of God. Hooker notes that the knowledge of God must be so imparted, because that knowledge is "the seed of whatsoever perfect virtue groweth from us. . . ." Herbert sees preaching as a way to turn knowledge "to reformation of life by pithy and lively exhortations." Wake holds the proper subject of catechesis to be, not theological speculation for its own sake, but the knowledge of whatever is necessary in order to serve God here and be saved hereafter. *The Whole Duty* chides the congregation to hear sermons "by putting useful instructions into practice." Hobart goes on to say that we should hear sermons to foster our "growth in holiness and virtue." These passages reflect the characteristic Anglican concern for the Christian life as one of growth into deeper relationship with God.

C. For Discussion

1. Our cultural understanding of preaching has been strongly influenced by the Great Awakenings and revivalism that came after most of the excerpts in Chapter Thirteen. How does revivalist preaching differ from the kind of preaching described in Chapter Thirteen? How are they similar?

2. The original model of catechetical instruction from the early church was a three-year course of instruction for adult converts to Christianity. Such instruction culminated in Baptism, and was followed by ongoing instruction in practices of the Church that could be revealed only to the Baptized. How was catechesis different in seventeenth-century England, both with regard to its social context and its theological function? How is it different today?

3. What do you consider to be the purpose of catechesis and preaching today? What should be included in catechetical instruction and sermons if they are to accomplish this purpose?

4. Some specialists in the field of Christian education are calling into question whether such education should be primarily a matter of imparting facts. They see the education project more in terms of such goals as building a sense of community or nurturing the individual Christian in a developmental process of achieving personal and spiritual maturity.[5] How is this approach similar to seventeenth-century Anglican catechesis with its emphasis on sanctification, the mercies of God, and the threat of punishment for sin? How is it different?

5. *The New Whole Duty Of Man* suggests that eighteenth-century congregations were at least as critical of preachers as modern congregations are. *The Whole Duty* prescribes humble attention to the sermon. What attitude do you consider to be appropriate for hearing a sermon? Is it different from a dramatic performance that one is expected to critique and review? Is it the Word of God that should be received reverently even if one considers the content of the sermon to be unreasonable and unorthodox?

6. What should be the role of parents in catechizing children? How does this relate to the domestic piety that was discussed in relation to marriage?

Conclusion

Prayer Book Spirituality is a collection of works by English and American writers reflecting on Anglican modes of prayer, sacraments, and spirituality over a period of some 300 years. The authors are separated by different historical contexts, cultural environments, and, sometimes, theological viewpoints. Yet these writers are bound by worship according to the tradition of *The Book Of Common Prayer* (albeit, some used different editions than others). This fact alone makes *Prayer Book Spirituality* an apt statement of central features of Anglicanism—of its life, of its prayer, and of its self-interpretation. Anglicans are a diverse people, perhaps more diverse than many other denominations. Not surprisingly, Anglicans therefore find much about which to disagree. Yet, the disagreements occur within a context of a shared liturgical life embodied in *The Book Of Common Prayer.*
 Stevick writes:

> . . . (The Book Of Common Prayer) *is a powerful, comprehensive, authoritative influence whose character has shaped all Anglican spirituality in all generations. Its phrases, balance of themes, and its tone become internalized. Its qualities impart themselves to those who habitually and sympathetically use it.* [1]

Indeed, it is the Prayer Book, rather than doctrinal confessions, that is definitive of Anglicanism. The Prayer Book is comprehensive in its application to Christian life from cradle to grave; and cohesive in that the prayers and rites interweave common themes throughout each of the steps in our pilgrimage. The domestic piety of marriage is the context for catechesis. The vows of the baptismal covenant structure

89

the self-examination for the Rite of Reconciliation. The assurance of God's love, which we experience in the Eucharist, is recalled as the ground of our hope in the burial service.

Most importantly *Prayer Book Spirituality* reflects the unitive power of God's presence and activity in our corporate life. As Stevick notes:

> *The Prayer Book speaks throughout in the plural: "we praise you . . . , we confess you . . . , we give thanks." The Prayer Book is the voice of a praying community, not a manual for private devotions. It is written for a collective life. . . . Corporate worship of the sort of the Prayer Book implies some theological, ecclesiological understandings. Life is communal. Redemption is communal. To be Christian is to exist in a body of close relationships.* [2]

We sincerely hope that your reflective study and devotional use of these classical reflections on the spiritual experience of Prayer Book worship will enrich your own growth in the Christian faith as you worship in the Prayer Book tradition.

Biographies of Authors[1]

Allestree, Richard (1619–1681), *Priest.* He served in the Royalist forces in the Civil War. During the Puritan Commonwealth, when worship according to *The Book of Common Prayer* was prohibited, he and J. Fell conducted Prayer Book services in a private home in Oxford. He is the author of *The Whole Duty Of Man.*

Andrewes, Lancelot (1555–1626), *Bishop of Winchester.* Andrewes was most famous for his "remarkable preaching." He was one of the principal influences in the formation of a "distinctive Anglican theology." Andrewes took a leading part at the Hampton Court Conference, and was one of the translators of the Authorized (King James) Version Of The Bible. He opposed Calvinism, and wanted the Church of England to express its worship in an "ordered ceremonial." Andrewes's greatest literary achievements include *Preces Privatae* and *Ninety-Six Sermons.* Commemoration date: September 26.

Beveridge, William (1637–1708), *Bishop Of St. Asaph.* Beveridge was a Greek scholar with "non-juring sympathies." He wrote an *Exposition of the Thirty-Nine Articles; Excelency and Usefulness of the Common Prayer;* and *Private Thoughts Upon Religion.* Beveridge conducted a daily service and celebrated the Eucharist weekly as vicar of St. Peter's, Cornhill. He was generally a High Churchman, but he embraced much of Calvin's teaching on predestination, and believed only a few people would be saved.

Bisse, Thomas (d. 1731), *Priest.* Bisse became preacher at Rolls Chapel, London in 1715. The next year, he was appointed to the chancellorship of Hereford Cathedral upon the removal of his nonjuror predecessor. He was a frequent and eloquent preacher, and several of his occasional sermons were published. His most famous sermons include "The Beauty of Holiness in the Common Prayer," "A Rationale on Cathedral Worship or Choir-Service," "Decency and Order in Public Worship," and "A Course of Sermons on the Lord's Prayer."[2]

Brevint, Daniel (1616–1695), *Dean of Lincoln.* Brevint is remembered chiefly as a polemical and devotional writer. He grew up on Jersey, but studied at the Protestant University of Saumur on the Loire. When he sought to pursue an academic career in England, his foreign degree was confirmed over the opposition of Archbishop Laud who distrusted such a Protestant background. Later the parliamentary commission deprived him of his Oxford fellowship. During the reign of the Puritans, he was forced to take refuge in France, where he served as minister to a Protestant Church. While in exile, Brevint became acquainted with Cosin and Durel, and was ordained to the priesthood. Also during this time, he attempted unsuccessfully to negotiate a settlement of differences between French Protestants and Roman Catholics. After the Restoration, Brevint returned to England and held various ecclesiastical positions, having the support of Cosin who was now Bishop of Durham. Brevint's writings are, for the most part, directed against the Church of Rome, which he criticized harshly after the failed negotiations in France. He was especially vehement in arguing points of Eucharistic theology.[3]

Brownell, Thomas (1779–1865), *Bishop of Connecticut.* Brownell was a classical languages scholar until his marriage to an ardent Episcopalian led him to a deeper study of theology that culminated in a call to ordained ministry. He had, for some time, questioned his family's Calvinism, and now accepted the scriptural and historical basis for episcopacy. Brownell was ordained by Hobart in 1811, and was consecrated bishop in 1819. He was the first president of Trinity College in Hartford. In 1852, he became Presiding Bishop. His *Commentary on the Book of Common Prayer* was highly regarded.[4]

Coleridge, Samuel Taylor (1772–1834), *Poet and theologian.* He taught the need for a spiritual interpretation of life. He was influenced by Unitarianism and pantheism in his youth. Coleridge denied any inherent conflict between modern science and Christianity. He conceded only pragmatic tests of faith, emphasizing the beneficent influence of Christianity on human life. He is known as "the Father Of The Broad Church Movement."

Comber, Thomas (1644–1699), *Dean of Durham.* Comber wrote in an effort to reconcile Protestant dissenters to the services of the Church of England. He resisted James II's attempt to fill Anglican benefices with Roman Catholics, and supported William and Mary.

Cosin, John (1594–1672), *Bishop Of Durham.* He was a friend of William Laud and at odds with the Puritan party. He was deprived of his benefices by the Long Parliament because of his "Popish innovations." Cosin spent the period of the Commonwealth in France, and returned to England at the Restoration in order to serve as Bishop of Durham. Cosin worked at reconciliation of the Church of England with Presbyterians, but remained an advocate of elaborate ritual. He used all the legal powers available to him to enforce conformity to the doctrine and practices of the Church of England. Cosin was one of the leading revisers at the Savoy Conference. Most of his writings are polemical.

Durel, John (1625–1683), *Dean of Windsor and Wolverhampton.* Durel served as chaplain to Charles II in 1662. He founded the Savoy French Episcopal Chapel and was its first minister. Durel's works include *The Liturgy Of The Church Of England; A View of the Government and Public Worship of God in the Reformed Churches beyond the Seas;* and *Sanctae Ecclesiae Anglicanae . . . Vindiciae.*

Hammond, Henry (1605–1660), *Priest.* Hammond became a priest at Penshurst, Kent in 1633. He instituted daily services and monthly celebrations of the Eucharist. Hammond was chaplain to Charles I until he was incarcerated in 1647 by Puritans. After being released, he lived privately until his death at Westwood, Worcestershire. His retirement was imposed by the 1655 decree forbidding Anglican clergy to exercise their ministry. He devoted himself to "relieving other deprived clergy" and raising money to train future ordinands. Hammond "maintained high standards of personal devotion and discipline."

Henshaw, J. P. K. (1792–1852), *Bishop of Rhode Island.* Henshaw, while an adolescent business man in Boston, was converted to the Episcopal church and the evangelical movement. He studied theology under Bishop Griswold and was ordained on his twenty-first birthday. Four years later he was called to St. Peter's, Baltimore, where he served for twenty-six years. In 1843 he became bishop of Rhode Island. Henshaw saw the patristic church as the model for his day, believing in its "immutable revealed truth and apostolically revealed order." He opposed Protestant sectarianism, Boston liberalism, and the Oxford Movement.[5]

Herbert, George (1593–1633), *Poet and priest.* Herbert pursued a career as a courtier until the death of James I foreclosed his court prospects. Nicholas Ferrar then encouraged him to study divinity. He was ordained in 1630 and spent his last years as rector of Fugglestone with Bemerton, near Salisbury. Herbert's most famous prose work is *A Priest To The Temple; or the Country Parson.* His collection of poems entitled *The Temple* was entrusted to Ferrar on Herbert's deathbed and was first published in 1633. Herbert's poetry later influenced the works of Henry Vaughn and Samuel Taylor Coleridge. Commemoration date: February 27.

Hobart, John Henry (1775–1830), *Bishop of New York.* Hobart became bishop of New York in 1811, at a time of "suspended animation" of the Episcopal Church following the American Revolution. Within his first four years as bishop, he doubled the number of clergy and quadrupled the number of missioners in his diocese. During his episcopacy, he "planted a church in almost every major town of New York State, and initiated missionary work among the Oneida Indians." Hobart was one of the founders of the General Theological Seminary, and he revived Geneva College, now Hobart College. Hobart established The Bible and Common Prayer Book Society of New York. He was a leader in producing theological and devotional manuals for the laity. He also influenced the Oxford Movement in England. Commemoration date: September 12.[6]

Hooker, Richard (1554?–1600), *Priest, Master Of The Temple.* Hooker is the "premier apologist for the Elizabethan Settlement." He won acclaim for championing the Anglican position in his controversy with Travers in 1584. Hooker wrote his classic *Treatise on the Laws of Ecclesiastical Polity* in the 1590s and portions were published posthumously. The purpose of the book was to defend episcopacy but, in doing so, Hooker developed a more comprehensive doctrine of natural law and human destiny that provided the framework for his arguments concerning church polity. Hooker stressed the doctrine of natural law as the expression of God's supreme reason. He saw the Church as an organic, not static, institution; and believed that polity could change according to circumstances. Thus the Church of England could be both reformed and in continuity with the Roman tradition. Hooker's theory of political society influenced future writers, particularly John Locke. Hooker's writings are chiefly polemical defenses of the Church Of England from Puritan criticism. Commemoration date: November 3.

Horneck, Anthony (1641–1697), *Vicar of All Saints, Oxford, and Prebendary of Exeter Cathedral.* A native of Bacharach on the Rhine, Horneck was born of Protestant parents and studied theology at Heidelberg, but he came to England c. 1661. He also served as chaplain to William III and as Prebendary of Westminster. He wrote a number of devotional books dealing especially with Holy Communion.

Jewel, John (1522–1571), *Bishop of Salisbury.* He was elected a fellow at Oxford in 1542. After 1547, through the influence of Peter Martyr, Jewel became a leader in the Reforming Party. Consequently, he was forced into exile during the reign of Mary, but he opposed Knox and the advanced Calvinists in Frankfurt during his exile. Jewel returned to England on the accession of Elizabeth I, and became bishop of Salisbury. Thereafter he supported the Elizabethan Settlement against both Roman Catholic and Puritan criticism. In 1564 he published the *Apologia Ecclesiae Anglicanae,* which defended Anglican claims. Jewel was a benefactor of the young Richard Hooker, and some of Jewel's teachings are reflected in Hooker's *Treatise on the Laws of Ecclesiastical Polity.*

Johnson, Samuel (1696–1772), *Priest and Missionary.* Johnson was a tutor at Collegiate School (Yale) in New Haven for three years. He then accepted the pastorate of a Congregational church near the college, and began studying theology and church history. This study led to his conversion to Anglicanism. Johnson thereupon went to England, where he was ordained and then sent back to Connecticut as an S.P.G. missionary. In 1724 he opened the first Anglican church building in Connecticut. He was a close friend of the English philosopher Berkeley, and espoused Berkeley's idealist philosophy. In 1754 Johnson became the first president of King's College, now Columbia University. Johnson wrote extensively in the field of philosophy. He is regarded, with Jonathan Edwards, as "one of the two most important exponents of idealist philosophy in colonial America."[7]

L'Estrange, Hamon (1605–1660), *Author.* He was admitted to Gray's Inn in 1617, but apparently was never called to the Bar. He supported the King in the Civil War. L'Estrange is the author of *God's Sabbath before and under the Law and under the Gospel; Reign of King Charles;* and *The Alliance of Divine Offices.*

Maurice, Frederick Dennison (1805–1872), *Priest and theologian.* Maurice grew up in a Unitarian household that became painfully divided over religious differences. He was an ardent student of the philosophy and theology of Samuel Taylor Coleridge even before he entered Cambridge, and, while a student, he defended Coleridge's teachings against utilitarianism. Maurice gradually accepted Anglicanism and was ordained in 1834. After the political unrest of 1848, Maurice became politically active. With J. M. Ludlow, he founded the Christian Socialist Movement. Later he founded the Working Men's College in London, where he promoted Christian Socialism. Maurice's greatest theological work was *The Kingdom of Christ.* He was a Broad Church theologian, and he argued that the atonement effected a redemption of humankind that was not contingent on right beliefs.[8] Commemoration date: April 1.

Nelson, Robert (1656–1715), *nonjuring layman.* Nelson strongly disapproved of the Revolution of 1688 and went abroad to avoid it. He returned to England in 1691 and became a nonjuror; however, he returned to the established Church in 1710. Nelson was a generous philanthropist, and supported the S.P.C.K. and the S.P.G. His *Companion for the Festivals and Fasts of the Church of England* enjoyed long-lasting popularity.

Patrick, Simon (1626–1707), *Bishop of Chichester and Ely.* While a student at Cambridge, Patrick was influenced by the Cambridge Platonists. He was ordained a Presbyterian minister; but after studying the works of Hammond and Thorndike, he sought and received Episcopal ordination. He helped to found the S.P.C.K. and also supported the S.P.G. He was a prolific writer, especially of controversial works disputing with Nonconformists and Roman Catholics.

Pearson, John (1613–1686), *Bishop of Chester.* Pearson was ordained in 1639, but was forced into semiretirement after he supported the Royalist cause in the Civil War. After the Restoration he held high academic posts, and was consecrated bishop in 1673. He is regarded as "one of the most erudite divines of a scholarly age." His classical *Exposition of the Creed* began as a series of lectures at St. Clement's, Eastcheap. Pearson wrote a number of other works, chiefly defending positions of the Church of England against Nonconformist and Roman criticism.

Seabury, Samuel (1729–1796), *First Bishop of the Protestant Episcopal Church Of America.* Seabury studied theology at Yale and medicine at Edinburgh before being ordained a priest by the bishop of Lincoln. He later came to the American colonies as a missionary. Seabury briefly suffered imprisonment as a result of a dispute with Alexander Hamilton. In 1783 he was elected bishop, but he could not be consecrated by English bishops as American independence precluded him from swearing the oath of allegiance to the king. The problem was resolved when Seabury was consecrated bishop by Scottish bishops. Seabury was highly regarded as an organizer and administrator and proved to be a pioneer of the Anglican Church in America. His consecration as bishop is commemorated on November 14.

Secker, Thomas (1693–1768), *Archbishop of Canterbury.* Secker's parents were dissenters and sent their son to a dissenters' academy for training to become a minister in that tradition. Secker, however, became doubtful about the dissenter doctrine and abandoned the study of divinity for the study of medicine in France. Through the influence of student friends, including Joseph Butler, Secker gradually came over to the Church of England. He received his M.D. degree in 1721 and was ordained in 1722. Thereafter, Secker became close to the royal family and pursued a distinguished ecclesiastical career. This career culminated in his ascendency to the See of Canterbury despite political differences that arose between Secker and the crown. He was "an orthodox eighteenth-century prelate" with "a typical horror of enthusiasm." Nonetheless, he did not regard the Methodist movement as a secession and was moderate in his treatment of Methodism. His writings are characterized by a "studied simplicity" of style, and he assisted in revision of Butler's major works.[9]

Simeon, Charles (1759–1836), *Priest.* Simeon was a leader of the Evangelical Revival Movement in England. He was educated at Cambridge, and was appointed vicar of Holy Trinity, Cambridge, in 1783. His evangelical ministry was met with early opposition in the university and in his congregation, but he ultimately won wide acceptance. Simeon became a leader of the missionary movement as well. Commemoration date: November 12.

Sparrow, Anthony (1612–1685), *Bishop of Norwich.* Sparrow was a Fellow at Cambridge until he was expelled by the Puritans in 1644. After the Restoration he was named archdeacon of Sudbury, and he played an important role in the revision of the Prayer Book in 1662. He served as bishop of Exeter before being translated to Norwich. Sparrow was a High Churchman. He is remembered for his *Rationale or Practical Exposition of the Book of Common Prayer,* published at least as early as 1657 and often reprinted. The object of this book was to show that the Church of England service was neither "old superstitious Roman dotage" nor "schismatically new."

Sutton, Christopher (c. 1565–1629), *Canon of Winchester and of Lincoln.* Sutton is remembered chiefly as a devotional writer. His most popular work was *Godly Meditations upon the Most Holy Sacrament of the Lord's Supper.* In that book, Sutton defended a doctrine of the Lord's presence in the Eucharist midway between transubstantiation and the teaching of Zwingli. He argued that consecration did not change the substance of the elements, but it radically altered their use. *Godly Meditations* was reissued in the nineteenth century by John Henry Newman, and was popular among Tractarians.

Taylor, Jeremy (1613–1667) *Bishop of Down and Connor.* Taylor is best known as a writer of devotional literature, particularly the classics *The Rule and Exercise of Holy Living* and *The Rule and Exercise of Holy Dying.* Taylor enjoyed the support of Archbishop Laud before the Long Parliament, and served as a chaplain to the Royalist Army during the Civil War. After the Royalist defeat he was imprisoned for a time, and then retired to Wales to serve as chaplain to Lord Carbery at Golden Grove. During this period Taylor wrote many of his greatest works. After the Restoration he became a bishop in Ireland. His episcopacy was marked by harsh disputes with both Presbyterians and Roman Catholics. Taylor's doctrine of the Eucharist is regarded by some as being "near to the Receptionist or Virtualist position," which he set in direct contrast to the Roman doctrine of transubstantiation. Commemoration date: April 13.

Thorndike, Herbert (1598–1672), *Priest and theologian.* Thorndike's greatest historical significance is as a theologian, though he was little read after his death until his works were repopularized in the nineteenth century by the Tractarians. Thorndike argued for a unified Christendom based on the first six General Councils, and he conceded a certain superiority to the pope with prescriptive rights over the Western Church. His eucharistic doctrine rejects the views of Zwingli, Calvin, and Luther, as well as transubstantiation. He contended that the mystical but objective presence of Christ is added to the elements, not by the Words of Institution, but by prayer. Thorndike also wrote on the relations between Church and State.

Wake, William (1657–1737), *Archbishop of Canterbury.* Wake held various ecclesiastical positions before becoming Archbishop in 1716. He had lived for a time in Paris and was acquainted with Gallicanism. From 1717 to 1720 he was involved in negotiations seeking a union between the Church of England and the Gallicans in France. Wake was in sympathy also with Nonconformists and advocated changes in the Prayer Book to accommodate their concerns. He is the author of *Principles of the Christian Religion,* a commentary on the catechism that was quite popular.[10]

Endnotes

Introduction

1. *The Study Of Anglicanism,* ed. Stephen Sykes and John Booty (Philadelphia: SPCK/Fortune Press, 1988).

2. *Anglican Spirituality,* ed. William Wolf (Wilton, CT: Morehouse-Barlow, 1982).

3. Alan Jones and Rachel Hosmer, *Living In The Spirit* (New York: Seabury Press, 1979).

4. Martin Thornton, *English Spirituality: An Outline Of Ascetical Theology According To The English Pastoral Tradition* (London: SPCK, 1963).

5. Leonel Mitchell, *Praying Shapes Believing: A Theological Commentary On The Book Of Common Prayer* (Chicago: Winston Press, 1985).

6. Evelyn Underhill, *Worship* (New York: Crossroad Publishing Co., 1986). ∎

CHAPTER ONE: *On Prayer In Common*

1. Augustine Of Hippo, *The City Of God,* trans. Henry Bettenson (London: Penguin Group, 1972), pp.1087–1091.

2. James A. Carpenter, *Nature & Grace* (New York: Crossroad Publishing Co., 1988), pp.76–84.

3. Daniel B. Stevick, "The Spirituality Of The Book Of Common Prayer," in *Anglican Spirituality* (see intro., n.2), pp.105–120.

4. Louis Weil, *Gathered To Pray* (Cambridge, MA: Cowley Publications, 1986).

5. Anglican-Lutheran Consultation, *The Niagra Report* (London: Partnership House, 1988); World Council Of Churches, *Baptism, Eucharist, And Ministry* (Geneva: World Council Of Churches, 1982).

CHAPTER TWO: *On Prayer From A Book*

(no notes)

CHAPTER THREE: *The Calendar and Liturgical Year*

1. Thomas J. Talley, *The Origins Of The Liturgical Year* (New York: Pueblo Publishing Co., 1986).

2. Peter Cobb, "The History Of The Christian Year," in *The Study Of Liturgy,* ed. Cheslyn Jones, Geoffrey Wainwright, Edward Yarnold, SJ (New York: Oxford University Press, 1978), pp.403–419.

3. Kevin Donovan, "The Sanctoral," in *The Study Of Liturgy,* pp.419–432.

4. Mitchell, (see intro., n.5), pp.13–34.

5. Tilden Edwards, *Spiritual Friend* (New York: Paulist Press, 1980).

6. Mircea Eliade, *The Sacred & The Profane,* trans. Willard R. Trask (New York: Harcourt Brace Jovanovich, 1959), pp.20–113.

7. James W. McClendon, Jr., *Biography As Theology* (Nashville: Abingdon Press, 1974), pp.170–215.

CHAPTER FOUR: *The Daily Office*

1. Mitchell (see intro., n.5), pp.35–36; G. J. Cumming, "The Divine Office: The First Three Centuries," in *The Study Of Liturgy* (see ch.3, n.2), pp.353–355; Dominic F. Scotto, *Liturgy Of The Hours* (Petersham: St. Bede's Publications, 1986), pp.3–32; Robert J. Taft, *The Liturgy Of The Hours In East And West* (Collegeville, MN: Liturgical Press, 1986), pp.297–299; W. Jardine Grisbrook, "The Formative Period: Cathedral And Monastic Offices," in *The Study Of Liturgy,* pp.362–367.

2. Taft, pp.299–310; J. D. Critchton, "The Office Of the Hours In The West: The Middle Ages," in *The Study of Liturgy,* pp.369–371; Scotto, pp.32–38; *Time Sanctified: The Book Of Hours In Medieval Life,* ed. Robert S. Wieck (New York: Braziller, 1988).

3. G. J. Cumming, *A History Of Anglican Liturgy* (Glasgow: University Press, 1969); G. J. Cumming, "The Office In The Church Of England," in *The Study*

Of Liturgy, pp.390–395; Marion J. Hatchett, "Prayer Books," in *The Study Of Anglicanism* (see intro., n.1), pp.121–129; Marion J. Hatchett, *Commentary On The American Prayer Book* (New York: Seabury Press, 1980).

4. Thornton (see intro., n.4), p.260.

5. *The Daily Office: A Guide For Individual And Group Recitation* (Alexandria: Associated Parishes, 1981).

6. Thornton, pp.261–278.

7. Thornton, p.275.

8. Dietrich Bonhoeffer, *Life Together,* trans. John W. Doberstein (New York: Harper, 1954)

9. Mitchell, pp.35–67.

10. A. M. Allchin, *Participation In God: A Forgotten Strand In The Anglican Tradition* (Wilton, CT: Morehouse-Barlow, 1988).

11. John Booty, "Contrition In Anglican Spirituality," in *Anglican Spirituality* (see intro., n.2), pp.25–48.

12. Simone Weil, *Waiting For God,* trans. Emma Craufurd (New York: Harper, 1951), pp.25, 216–267.

13. Ann Belford Ulanov and Barry Ulanov, *Primary Speech: A Psychology Of Prayer* (Atlanta: John Knox Press, 1982).

CHAPTER FIVE: *The Litany*

1. Underhill (see intro., n.6), p.100.

2. Byron D. Stuhlman, *Prayer Book Rubrics Expanded* (New York: Church Hymnal Corp., 1987), p.53. The 1979 Prayer Book expands the Prayers of the People to be generally inclusive of the needs of the world. However Stuhlman's point underlines the classical importance of the Litany as the Church's prayer that is most inclusive of the world.

3. Mitchell (see intro., n.5), p.66. The Litany is also appropriate for use in an outdoor procession on Rogation Days. Stuhlman, p.54.

4. Stuhlman, p.53.

5. Mitchell, p.66.

6. Ulanov (see ch.4, n.13), pp.13–25, 51–62.

7. Underhill, pp.150–153; Ulanov, pp.85–97. On the subject of prayer for enemies, see Ulanov, pp.62–72.

CHAPTER SIX: *Christian Initiation*

1. For a historical background of Christian initiation rites, see K. W. Noakes, "From New Testament Times Until St. Cyprian"; E. J. Yarnold, "The Fourth And Fifth Centuries"; J. D. C. Fisher and E. J. Yarnold, "The West From About 500 A.D. To The Reformation"; and J. D. C. Fisher, "Lutheran, Anglican, and Reformed Rites" in *The Study Of Liturgy* (see ch.3, n.2), pp.80–118, 120–132. The foregoing sources may be more technical or academic than necessary, depending on the depth of inquiry desired. However, an excellent account of the theology of Cranmer's reform of the initiation rite and the theological and social forces that led to the modern revision is readily accessible in David R. Holeton, "Initiation," in *The Study Of Anglicanism* (see intro., n.1), pp.261–272.

2. Alec R. Vidler, *Witness To The Light: F. D. Maurice's Message For Today* (New York: Scribner's, 1948), pp.88–114.

3. Louis Weil, *Christian Initiation: A Theological And Pastoral Commentary On The Proposed Rites* (Alexandria, VA: Associated Parishes, 1977).

4. Mitchell (see intro., n.5), pp.88–127. See also, Stuhlman, *Prayer Book Rubrics Expanded*, pp.109–121.

5. *Baptism, Eucharist, and Ministry* (see ch.1, n.5), pp.2–7.

6. Eliade (see ch.3, n.6), pp.129–138.

CHAPTER SEVEN: *The Holy Eucharist*

1. Associated Parishes, *Parish Eucharist* (Alexandria, VA: Associated Parishes, 1977); Associated Parishes, *Holy Eucharist Rite II: A Commentary* (Alexandria: Associated Parishes, 1976).

2. *Baptism, Eucharist, And Ministry*, pp.10–15.

3. Underhill (see intro., n.6), p.138.

4. Mitchell, pp.128–185.

5. Berkhoff, *Christian Faith: An Introduction To The Study Of The Faith*, trans. Sierd Woudstra (Grand Rapids: Eerdman's, 1979), pp.369–371.

6. John Koenig, *New Testament Hospitality: Partnership With Strangers As Promise And Mission* (Philadelphia: Fortress Press, 1985).

7. Justin Martyr, *The First Apology*, ed. and trans. E. R. Hardy, in *Early Christian Fathers*, ed. Cyril C. Richardson (New York: Macmillan, 1970); Noakes,

"From The Apostolic Fathers To Irenaeus," in *The Study Of Liturgy* (see ch.3, n.2), pp.170–172.

8. J. Robert Wright, "Notes on the History of Worship," (unpublished manuscript), pp.4–5, 9–10.

9. A fine, brief summary of some of these developments may be found in Francis Oakley's *The Western Church In the Later Middle Ages* (Ithaca: Cornell University Press, 1979), pp.82–85. See also, Wright, pp.4–5, 9–10.

10. R. T. Beckwith, "The Anglican Eucharist: From Reformation To Restoration," in *The Study of Liturgy*, pp.263–271; Alan Dunstan, "The Eucharist In Anglicanism After 1662," in *The Study Of Liturgy*, pp.272–277. These sources may be more technical and scholarly than appropriate for a course surveying such a broad topic as Prayer Book spirituality. For a less technical account of Anglican eucharistic theology, see William R. Crockett, "Holy Communion," in *The Study Of Anglicanism* (see intro., n.1), pp.272–285. The best concise account of the historical development of Anglican eucharistic theology appears in Byron Stuhlman's, *Eucharistic Celebration 1789–1979* (New York: Church Hymnal Corp., 1988), pp.1–25.

11. Article 28 of the Articles Of Religion, *The Book Of Common Prayer*, p.873. See also Articles 29–31, which add important features to the Anglican doctrine.

12. Ibid, Article 29.

13. In our day, some Anglicans have urged the acceptance of a doctrine of transignification, which is also embraced by some Roman Catholic theologians. See e.g., John Macquarrie, *Principles Of Christian Theology* (New York: Scribner's, 1966), pp.479–481.

14. J. Robert Wright, "Notes On The History Of Worship," (unpublished manuscript), p.2.

CHAPTER EIGHT: *Marriage*

1. Philip Turner, "Limited Engagements," in *Men & Women*, ed. Philip Turner (Cambridge, MA: Cowley Publications, 1989), p.57.

2. Kenneth W. Stevenson, *Nuptial Blessing: A Study Of Christian Marriage Rites* (New York: Oxford University Press, 1983).

3. Associated Parishes, *The Celebration And Blessing Of A Marriage: A Liturgical And Pastoral Commentary* (Alexandria: Associated Parishes, 1987). Stuhlman, *Prayer Book Rubrics Expanded*, pp.153–148.

4. Mitchell (see intro., n.5), pp.189–197.

5. *Men & Women,* see note 1, above.

CHAPTER NINE: *Reconciliation of a Penitent*

1. Thornton (see intro., n.4), pp.149–155.

2. Underhill (see intro., n.6), p.338.

3. Mitchell, pp.200–207.

4. P. D. Butterfield, *How To Make Your Confession: A Primer For Members Of The Church Of England* (London: SPCK, 1952). See also, Martin L. Smith, *Reconciliation: Preparing For Confession* (Cambridge, MA: Cowley Press, 1985).

CHAPTER TEN: *Ministry to the Sick*

1. Morton T. Kelsey, *Psychology, Medicine, and Christian Healing* (San Francisco: Harper & Row, 1988) pp.41–174.

2. Ibid, p.174.

3. Mitchell, p.207.

4. Ibid, p.207.

5. Elizabeth Kubler-Ross, *On Death And Dying* (New York: MacMillan, 1969).

6. Mary Jane Linn, Dennis Linn, and Matthew Linn, *Healing The Dying* (New York: Paulist Press, 1979).

7. Francis MacNutt, *Healing* (Notre Dame, IN: Ave Maria Press, 1974), pp.248–261.

CHAPTER ELEVEN: *The Burial of the Dead*

1. "Purgatory," *Oxford Dictionary Of The Christian Church,* ed. F. L. Cross and E. A. Livingstone (London: Oxford University Press, 1984), pp.1044–1045.

2. Lewis W. Spitz, *The Protestant Reformation: 1517–1559* (New York: Harper & Row, 1985), p.265.

3. Mitchell (see intro., n.5), 229.

4. Ibid, 224.

5. Associated Parishes, *The Burial Of The Dead: A Commentary* (Alexandria: Associated Parishes, 1980).

6. Augustine of Hippo (see ch.1, n.1), pp.1052–1068.

CHAPTER TWELVE: *Ordination*

1. Mark 1:16–20; 10:35–45.

2. I Corinthians 12:27–31; Acts 14:23.

3. I Timothy 3:1–16. For a further description of the ordering of ministry and of the ministerial roles in the New Testament, see Frank Hawkins, "Orders And Ordination In The New Testament," in *The Study Of Liturgy* (see ch.3, n.2), pp.290–297.

4. Williston Walker, Richard A. Norris, David W. Lotz, and Robert T. Handy, *A History Of The Christian Church* (New York: Scribner's, 1985) pp.45–50; 98–100; 183–187; "Orders" in *The Oxford Dictionary Of The Christian Church*, pp.1004–1006. Frank Hawkins, "The Tradition Of Ordination In The Second Century To The Time Of Hippolytus," in *The Study Of Liturgy*, pp.297–301. The threefold order was elaborated in the Middle Ages to allow for minor orders including subdeacons, acolytes, lectors, etc., to constitute seven orders and this number was held to have mystical and symbolic importance. J. H. Crehan, "Medieval Ordinations," in *The Study Of Liturgy*, p.324.

5. Paul F. Bradshaw, "Ordinals," in *The Study Of Anglicanism* (see intro., n.1), pp.143–153; John B. Webster, "Ministry And Priesthood," in *The Study Of Anglicanism*, pp.287–288; Paul F. Bradshaw, "Reformation Churches," in *The Study Of Liturgy*, pp.331–341.

6. Webster, "Ministry And Priesthood," pp.289–290.

7. O. C. Edwards, "Anglican Pastoral Tradition," in *The Study Of Anglicanism*, p.340.

8. Ibid, pp.340–341.

9. Webster, p.286.

10. Ibid, p.291.

11. Edwards, p.341.

12. Webster, pp.293–295.

13. *Baptism, Eucharist, And Ministry* (see ch.1, n.5), pp.20–32.

14. Richard Hooker, *Of The Lawes Of Ecclesiasticall Politie*, Book IV, in *The Complete Works Of Richard Hooker*, ed. W. Speed Hill, Vol. I (Cambridge: Belknap Press of Harvard University Press, 1977), p.278.

CHAPTER THIRTEEN: *Catechetical Instruction and Preaching*

1. Webster, p.286.

2. Mitchell (see intro., n.5), pp.1335–136; Stuhlman (see ch.5, n.2), p.71.

3. Thornton (see intro., n.4), pp.236–243.

4. Edwards, p.345.

5. For an example of the community building model, see Maria Harris, *Fashion Me A People: Curriculum In The Church* (Louisville: John Knox Press, 1989). The theological, psychological, and pedagogical text that has most influenced Christian education toward a model of nurturing Christians as they move along a developmental course consisting of distinct stages is James Fowler's *Stages Of Faith: The Psychology Of Human Development And The Quest For Meaning* (New York: Harper & Row, 1981).

CONCLUSION

1. Stevick (see ch.1, n.3), p.107.

2. Ibid, pp.114–115.

APPENDIX: *Biographies of Authors*

1. Except where otherwise noted, the biographical data in this appendix is derived from the *Oxford Dictionary of the Christian Church*, ed. F. L. Cross and E. A. Livingstone (New York: Oxford University Press, 1983) and from P. E. More and F. L. Cross, *Anglicanism* (London: *SPCK*, 1951). The commemoration days, for those authors who are remembered in the liturgical calendar, are noted in *Lesser Feasts And Fasts*, ed. Charles M. Guilbert (New York: Church Hymnal Corp., 1988).

2. "Bisse, Thomas," *A Dictionary of National Biography*, ed. Sir Leslie Stephen and Sir Sidney Lee (London: Oxford University Press, 1960), Vol. II, p.560.

3. "Brevint, Daniel," *A Dictionary of National* Biography, Vol. II, pp.1198–1199.

4. "Brownell, Thomas," *Dictionary of American Biography*, ed. Allen Johnson (New York: Scribner's, 1929), Vol. III, pp.171–172.

5. Dudley Tyng, *Rhode Island Episcopalians 1635–1953* (Providence: Little Rhody Press, 1954), pp.21–28.

6. "Hobart, John Henry," *Lesser Feasts and Fasts,* p.330.

7. "Johnson, Samuel," *Dictionary of American Biography,* Vol. X, pp.118–119.

8. Alec R. Vidler, *Witness to the Light: F. D. Maurice's Message for Today* (New York: Scribner's, 1948).

9. "Secker, Thomas," *Dictionary of National Biography,* Vol. VII, pp.1108–1111.

10. See also Stephen Neill, *Anglicanism* (London: Mowbray & Co., 1958), pp.199–201.

Table of Sources

Cross, F. L. and Livingstone, E. A., eds. *The Oxford Dictionary Of The Christian Church.* London: Oxford University Press, 1984.

Cumming, G. J. "The Divine Office: The First Three Centuries." In *The Study Of Liturgy.* Edited by Cheslyn Jones, Geoffrey Wainwright, and Edward Yarnold. New York: Oxford University Press, 1978.

————. *A History Of The Anglican Liturgy.* Glasgow: The University Press, 1969.

————. "The Office Of The Church Of England." In *The Study Of Liturgy.* Edited by Cheslyn Jones, Geoffrey Wainwright, and Edward Yarnold. New York: Oxford University Press, 1978.

Donovan, Kevin. "The Sanctoral." In *The Study Of Liturgy.* Edited by Cheslyn Jones, Geoffrey Wainwright, and Edward Yarnold. New York: Oxford University Press, 1978.

Dunstan, Alan. "The Eucharist In Anglicanism After 1662." *In The Study Of Liturgy.* Edited by Cheslyn Jones, Geoffrey Wainwright, and Edward Yarnold. New York: Oxford University Press, 1978.

Edwards, O. C. "Anglican Pastoral Tradition." In *The Study Of Anglicanism.* Edited by Stephen Sykes and John Booty. Philadelphia: SPCK/Fortress Press, 1988.

Edwards, Tilden. *Spiritual Friend.* New York: Paulist Press, 1980.

Eliade, Mircea. *The Sacred & The Profane.* Translated by Willard R. Trask. New York: Harcourt Brace Jovanovich, 1959.

Fisher, J. D. C. "Lutheran, Anglican, And Reformed Rites." In *The Study Of Liturgy.* Edited by Cheslyn Jones, Geoffrey Wainwright, and Edward Yarnold. New York: Oxford University Press, 1978.

Fowler, James. *Stages Of Faith: The Psychology Of Human Development And The Quest For Meaning.* New York: Harper & Row, 1981.

Grisbrock, Jardine. "The Formative Period: Cathedral And Monastic Offices." In *The Study Of Liturgy.* Edited by Cheslyn Jones, Geoffrey Wainwright, and Edward Yarnold. New York: Oxford University Press, 1978.

Guilbert, Charles M., ed. *Lesser Feasts And Fasts.* New York: Church Hymnal Corp., 1988.

Harris, Maria. *Fashion Me A People: Curriculum In The Church.* Louisville: John Knox Press, 1989.

Hatchett, Marion. *Commentary On The American Prayer Book.* New York: Seabury Press, 1980.

———. "Prayer Books." In *The Study Of Anglicanism.* Edited by Stephen Sykes and John Booty. Philadelphia: SPCK/Fortress Press, 1988.

Hawkins, Frank. "Orders And Ordination In The New Testament." In *The Study Of Liturgy.* Edited by Cheslyn Jones, Geoffrey Wainwright, and Edward Yarnold. New York: Oxford University Press, 1978.

———. "The Tradition Of Ordination In The Second Century To The Time Of Hippolytus." In *The Study Of Liturgy.* " Edited by Cheslyn Jones, Geoffrey Wainwright, and Edward Yarnold. New York: Oxford University Press, 1978.

Hooker, Richard. *Of the Lawes Of Ecclesiasticall Politie.* In *The Complete Works Of Richard Hooker.* Edited by W. Speed Hill. Cambridge: Belknap Press of Harvard University Press, 1977.

Johnson, Alan, ed. *Dictionary Of American Biography.* New York: Scribner's, 1929.

Jones, Alan and Hosmer, Rachel. *Living In The Spirit.* New York: Seabury Press, 1979.

Kelsey, Morton T. *Psychology, Medicine, And Christian Healing.* San Francisco: Harper & Row, 1988.

Koenig, John. *New Testament Hospitality: Partnership With Strangers As Promise And Mission.* Philadelphia: Fortress Press, 1985.

Kubler-Ross, Elizabeth. *On Death And Dying.* New York: Macmillan, 1969.

Linn, Mary Jane; Linn, Dennis; and Linn, Matthew. *Healing The Dying.* New York: Paulist Press, 1979.

McClendon, James. *Biography As Theology.* Nashville: Abingdon Press, 1974.

MacNutt, Francis. *Healing.* Notre Dame: Ave Maria Press, 1974.

Macquarrie, John. *Principles Of Christian Theology.* New York: Scribner's, 1966.

Martyr, Justin. *The First Apology.* Translated by E. R. Hardy. In *Early Christian Fathers.* Edited by Cyril C. Richardson. New York: Macmillan, 1970.

Mitchell, Leonel. *Praying Shapes Believing: A Theological Commentary On The Book Of Common Prayer.* Chicago: Winston Press, 1985.

More, P. E. and Cross, F. L., eds. *Anglicanism.* Philadelphia: SPCK, 1951.

Neill, Stephen. *Anglicanism.* London: Mowbray & Co., Ltd., 1958.

Noakes, K. W. "From New Testament Times To St. Cyprian." In *The Study Of Liturgy.* Edited by Cheslyn Jones, Geoffrey Wainwright, and Edward Yarnold. New York: Oxford University Press, 1978.

————. "From The Apostlic Fathers To Irenaeus." In *The Study Of Liturgy.* Edited by Cheslyn Jones, Geoffrey Wainwright, and Edward Yarnold. New York: Oxford University Press, 1978.

Oakley, Francis. *The Western Church In The Later Middle Ages.* Ithaca: Cornell University Press, 1979.

Scotto, Dominic. *Liturgy Of The Hours.* Petersham: St. Bede's Publications, 1986.

Smith, Martin L. *Reconciliation: Preparing For Confession.* Cambridge, MA: Cowley Press, 1985.

Spitz, Lewis W. *The Protestant Reformation: 1517–1559.* New York: Harper & Row, 1985.

Stephen, Sir Leslie and Lee, Sir Sidney, eds. *A Dictionary Of National Biography.* London: Oxford University Press, 1960.

Stephenson, Kenneth W. *Nuptial Blessing: A Study Of Christian Marriage Rites.* New York: Oxford University Press, 1983.

Stevick, Daniel A. "The Spirituality Of The Book Of Common Prayer." In *Anglican Spirituality.* Edited by William Wolf. Wilton, CT: Morehouse-Barlow, 1982.

Stuhlman, Byron D. *Eucharistic Celebration 1789–1979.* New York: Church Hymnal Corp., 1988.

————. *Prayer Book Rubrics Expanded.* New York: Church Hymnal Corp., 1987.

Sykes, Stephen and Booty, John, eds. *The Study Of Anglicanism.* Philadelphia: SPCK/Fortress Press, 1988.

Talley, Thomas J. *The Origins Of The Liturgical Year.* New York: Pueblo Publishing Co., 1986.

Thornton, Martin. *English Spirituality: An Outline Of Ascetical Theology According To The English Pastoral Tradition.* London: SPCK, 1963.

Turner, Philip. "Limited Engagements." In *Men & Women.* Edited by Philip Turner. Cambridge, MA: Cowley Publications, 1984.

Tyng, Dudley. *Rhode Island Episcopalians 1635–1953.* Providence: Little Rhody Press, 1954.

Ulanov, Ann Belford, and Ulanov, Barry. *Primary Speech: A Psychology Of Prayer.* Atlanta: John Knox Press, 1982.

Underhill, Evelyn. *Worship.* New York: Crossroad Publishing Co., 1986.

Vidler, Alec. *Witness To The Light: F. D. Maurice's Message For Today.* New York: Scribner's, 1948.

Walker, Williston; Norris, Richard A.; Lotz, David W.; and Handy, Robert T. *A History Of The Christian Church.* New York: Scribner's, 1985.

Webster, John B. "Ministry And Priesthood." In *The Study Of Anglicanism.* Edited by Stephen Sykes and John Booty. Philadelphia: SPCK/Fortress Press, 1988.

Weick, Robert S., ed. *Time Sanctified: The Book Of Hours In Medieval Life.* New York: Braziller, 1988.

Weil, Louis. *Christian Initiation: A Theological And Pastoral Commentary On the Proposed Rites.* Alexandria: Associated Parishes, 1977.

———. *Gathered To Pray.* Cambridge, MA: Cowley Publications, 1986.

Weil, Simone. *Waiting For God.* Translated by Emma Craufurd. New York: Harper, 1951.

Wright, J. Robert. "Notes On The History Of Worship." (unpublished manuscript).

———. *Prayer Book Spirituality.* New York: Church Hymnal Corp., 1989.

Yarnold, E. J. "The Fourth And Fifth Centuries." In *The Study Of Liturgy.* Edited by Cheslyn Jones, Geoffrey Wainwright, and Edward Yarnold. New York: Oxford University Press, 1978.